• Dog Breed Handbooks •

German Shepherd

• DOG BREED HANDBOOKS •

GERMAN SHEPHERD

DR. BRUCE FOGLE

SPECIAL PHOTOGRAPHY BY
TRACY MORGAN

A DK PUBLISHING BOOK
www.dk.com

Project Editor JILL FORNARY
Art Editor SARAH GOODWIN
Editor SARAH LILLICRAPP
Designer WENDY BARTLET
Managing Editor FRANCIS RITTER
Managing Art Editor DEREK COOMBES
DTP Designer CRESSIDA JOYCE
Picture Researcher JO CARLILL
Production Controller ADRIAN GATHERCOLE
US Editor SALLY A. ROSE

First American Edition, 1996
First published as a Dorling Kindersley paperback 1999
2 4 6 8 10 9 7 5 3 1

Published in the United States by DK Publishing, Inc.,
95 Madison Avenue, New York, New York 10016

First published in Great Britain in 1996
by Dorling Kindersley Limited,
9 Henrietta Street, London WC2E 8PS

Library of Congress Cataloging-in-Publication Data

Fogle, Bruce
  German shepherd / by Bruce Fogle. - - 1st American ed.
  p.   cm. - - (Dog breed handbooks)
  Includes index.
  ISBN 0-7894-0568-7
  ISBN 0-7894-4194-2 pbf
  1. German shepherd dog. I. Title. II. Series : Fogle, Bruce. Dog
breed handbooks.
  SF429 - G37 F67 1996
  636.7'37- -dc20
                              95 - 44069
                              CIP
                              r98

Reproduced by Colourscan, Singapore
Printed in Hong Kong by Wing King Tong

CONTENTS

INTRODUCTION

MANY CENTURIES of evolution have produced today's domestic dog breeds from their common wolf ancestor. Over 15,000 years ago, when our ancient relatives first created semipermanent settlements, local wolves in turn moved into the areas surrounding the encampments to scavenge for food. Only the smallest and tamest of these "self-domesticated" wolves survived, and within a very short time the modified wolf-dog had emerged.

Although the German Shepherd looks similar to its distant relative, the wolf, it exhibits a far more tractable character

The early human settlers, recognizing potential uses for these creatures, began capturing young cubs and raising them to protect their campsites and assist in hunting.

ADAPTATION OF THE BREED

By about 6,000 years ago, selective breeding by humans had produced many different dog breeds with enhanced qualities for specific roles, including guarding, load-bearing, and hunting. The development of agriculture demanded yet another canine ability, to guard and herd livestock. Careful mating of those dogs that excelled at this hard work produced numerous herding breeds throughout Europe, varying in physical characteristics. It is from this genetic "soup" that the modern German Shepherd eventually emerged – not by chance, but through highly selective breeding. Although today few German Shepherds are used as herders, these refined origins have made them among the most versatile and trainable of all dogs.

Selective breeding has increased the fertility of dogs, yielding larger litters than those of their wolf ancestors

Ever alert and always keen to serve, the German Shepherd is justly renowned for its obedience and loyalty

Its authoritative bark and protective inclination to guard and defend home territory make the German Shepherd an effective security dog

NATURAL PROTECTIVE INSTINCTS

The German Shepherd is not by nature particularly aggressive, ranking average compared with other dog breeds. Yet the Shepherd has been specifically bred not only for supreme responsiveness to command but to retain its instinctive canine disposition to guard and protect. This combination has made it the world's most successful security dog.

THE IDEAL COMPANION

Its adaptability and alertness have made the German Shepherd a favorite service breed – Shepherds were the first guide dogs for the blind and are now also used in all types of rescue work, the detection of drugs and explosives, and in many other assistance and police roles. The dog's exceptional qualities have even taken it to Hollywood, where Rin Tin Tin was the first internationally famous canine film star. But for many devotees

As its name suggests, the Shepherd has a natural herding instinct, which stems from its original working role

of the breed, the German Shepherd's most outstanding characteristic is its loyal dedication to its owner – making it the perfect companion dog, and surely destined to grow ever more popular worldwide.

Superb responsiveness to training, noble features, and an unsurpassed service record ensure that the German Shepherd is one of the most celebrated and popular of breeds

THE IDEAL CHOICE

THE GERMAN SHEPHERD is indeed an impressive breed – noble and handsome in appearance, highly alert, and always full of life. However, before choosing a Shepherd either for showing or as a pet, make sure that you are the right owner for such an energetic and spirited dog.

LOYAL PROTECTOR OF THE HOME

Most dogs are kept primarily as companions, but even the smallest can also provide security through its vigilance and keen senses. Because of its imposing size, looks, and protective, ever-alert nature, the German Shepherd is virtually ideal as a guard dog. But its behavior must be socially acceptable – good training and early interaction with other animals is vital.

DOGS ARE NOT WEAPONS

Pet Shepherds may be trained to bark on command and to guard, but should never be taught to attack. Inappropriate training for aggression denigrates the breed, presenting an unfair image to the general public and potential owners. Because mature German Shepherds can be physically intimidating, their handling carries special responsibilities.

BOUNDING WITH ENERGY

German Shepherds are large dogs that thrive on physical and mental activity. Consider acquiring one only if you can provide it with the space, exercise, and attention it needs. Bored Shepherds lead unhappy lives, and through frustration may tend to be vocal and even destructive. Properly cared for, this vigorous, responsive breed can be among the most rewarding of all dogs to own.

Play is integral part of relationship between dog and owner

"PERFECTION" OR PERSONALITY?

While breeders may try to produce show-quality dogs that conform as closely as possible to the official standard set for the breed, each individual will deviate in certain ways from the ideal. However, a winning character is certainly the most important quality for a good companion, and idiosyncratic features are often endearing.

Puppy has lopped ear which will probably, but not necessarily, straighten out

AN AFFABLE, OBEDIENT COMPANION

Well-trained Shepherd interacts happily with strangers and other animals

Obedience comes naturally to German Shepherds, but it is only through dedicated training that a dog becomes a truly satisfying companion. From the moment you become an owner, you will need to invest time, introducing your Shepherd to new situations and always teaching good conduct. A friendly, well-mannered dog is a pleasure both for you and others.

CARED FOR AS ONE OF THE FAMILY

A dog can provide an enormous amount of companionship and affection, but you must be prepared to care for your pet for at least the next 13 years. Like a young child, it depends on you for its health and well-being. Make sure you can cope with inconveniences such as house training and shedding hair, as well as the expense of food and veterinary attention.

Dog enriches family life, but is totally reliant on you

BREED CHARACTERISTICS

THE BEAUTIFULLY PROPORTIONED German Shepherd has a powerful, supple body reflecting its development as a versatile working dog. Alert, tractable, and steady in character, the Shepherd is dedicated to its master and composed with strangers. A resilient spirit, calm self-confidence, and superb looks are among the qualities that distinguish this fine breed.

WATCHFULLY ATTENTIVE

Good breeding emphasizes a calm, tractable, and trustworthy nature as well as noble looks and physical strength. The keen, alert Shepherd shows great devotion and loyalty.

MUSCULAR AND WELL BALANCED

A slightly long body in relation to height gives the breed a far-reaching, elegant gait. The German Shepherd's powerful yet agile physique and tireless, responsive spirit make it a superbly adaptable working dog as well as a fine, dutiful companion.

DOUBLE COAT
Hard, dense, weather-resistant outer coat covers thick, woolly insulating down

BACK
Straight and strong; top line of body is long and flowing, sloping gently downward toward hindquarters

TAIL
Bushy and long, hanging in saberlike curve when at rest and raised when trotting

HINDQUARTERS
Powerful, broad, and well muscled, and angled in proportion to forequarters, producing a balanced gait

FEET
Rounded, with amply cushioned, durable pads; toes well closed and arched, with strong, dark nails

SKULL
In perfect proportion to body, fairly broad between ears, with forehead only moderately domed, and blending into muzzle without too pronounced an indentation

INTERPRETING THE OFFICIAL BREED STANDARD

The written "ideal," or breed standard, describing the German Shepherd's appearance and behaviour, remains virtually identical worldwide, yet the way this standard is interpreted by breeders and judges varies. Certain trends, however, have emerged over time, with Shepherds gradually increasing in size; today, they are considerably larger and with a more sloping top contour than when the standard was first devised. Despite these modifications, the standard has always continued to emphasize a sound temperament and working ability along with physical beauty.

EARS
Medium-sized, broad at base tapering to pointed tips, carried erect

NATURAL BEAUTY AND LIVELY SPIRIT
Erect ears and a well-proportioned muzzle give the head a natural, wolflike appearance. Masculinity and femininity are clearly defined, with the expression bright and calmly assured.

EYES
Almond-shaped, usually dark, expressing a lively, self-assured nature

MUZZLE
Wedge-shaped and strong, about half total length of skull, with firm lips

FOREQUARTERS
Shoulder blades are long, set obliquely, and laid flat to body; length of forelegs exceeds depth of chest

JAWS AND TEETH
Strongly developed, with upper teeth closely overlapping lower teeth

BODY
Fairly deep chest, with oval ribs never extending below elbows, to allow free movement; belly firm and only slightly drawn up

MEASUREMENTS (AMERICAN BREED STANDARD)
Height at withers (see page 77):
FEMALE 22–24 in (56–61 cm)
MALE 24–26 in (61–66 cm)
Weight, in proportion to height:
FEMALE 66–88 lb (30–40 kg)
MALE 75–99 lb (34–45 kg)

6 ft (1.5 m)

BEHAVIOR PROFILE

EVERY DOG HAS ITS OWN personality, molded in part by its experiences within the litter, and later with you. Heredity is the other important factor, bringing both positive and negative traits for each breed. Overall, the German Shepherd's devoted, spirited character has made it an enduring favorite.

TRAINABILITY/OBEDIENCE

Shepherds are very responsive to training, and typically show great loyalty and obedience to their owners. Only the Labrador Retriever and the Australian Cattle Dog, breeds also specifically developed to work under human direction, are considered more trainable.

PLAYFULNESS WITH OTHER DOGS

Despite a reputation for mild aloofness with other dogs, German Shepherds are more playful than many breeds, actively enjoying friendly interaction with fellow canines. A lively character and natural inquisitiveness make them in fact a rather sociable breed.

BARKING TO PROTECT THE HOME

The alert Shepherd is an ever-vigilant house guard. While Dachshunds, Lhasa Apsos, and Toy Poodles do just as much protective barking, the Shepherd may also put up a defensive presence. Only the Australian Cattle Dog is less likely to accept intruders.

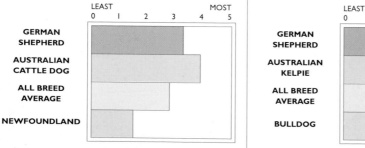

NEED FOR PHYSICAL ACTIVITY

A large, energetic dog bred for work, the Shepherd thrives on physical and mental activity. Only the Australian Kelpie and Cattle Dog and Chesapeake Bay Retriever have a greater need, although early experience influences this trait even more than genetics.

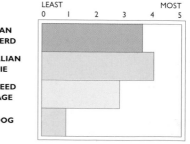

How to Use the Behavior Charts

In a recent study, experienced vets and dog breeders have assessed over 100 breeds, rating each on a scale of 0–5 for specific personality traits, with 0 representing the lowest score among all dogs and 5 the highest. Here, for eight different behaviors, the German Shepherd is compared with the statistically "average" canine, as well as the breeds reported at both extremes for each characteristic. Note that these findings do not take into consideration either sex or coat color.

Reliable with Strange Children

German Shepherds are just as dependable with unfamiliar children as the "average" dog, similar to breeds such as the Shih Tzu and Keeshond. Even so, an adult should always be present, and children, until emotionally mature, should never be left alone with any dog.

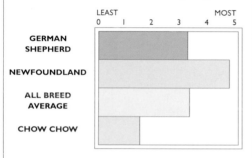

Calm in New Circumstances

In this highly inherited trait, Shepherds are just below average, tending to be slightly nervous or fearful in strange situations, but less so than some smaller breeds. This can be diminished through selective breeding of more relaxed personalities, and gentle training.

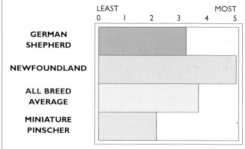

Nondestructive when Alone

Regarding destructiveness when left alone, Shepherds are just below dog "average," about the same as Dachshunds, Schnauzers, and West Highland Terriers. In Shepherds, scratching on walls, digging in carpets or gardens, or barking when alone usually indicate anxiety or worry.

House Trainable

Virtually all dogs respond fairly well to house training, but the German Shepherd and the Labrador Retriever are rated as the most receptive, reflecting both breeds' aptitude for learning, general eagerness to please, and exceptionally willing, dutiful natures.

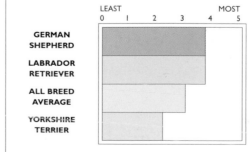

COATS AND COLORS

THE TYPICAL GERMAN SHEPHERD is black with tan or gold markings, yet they can also be all black, white, or sable — with black-tipped hairs on tan, gold, gray, or silver. White and long-haired dogs are frowned upon in the show ring. Curiously, coat color may have a slight bearing on personality.

WIDE-RANGING COLORATIONS

The developer of the modern German Shepherd, Max von Stephanitz, wrote wisely: "No good dog can be a bad color." In practice, however, black-and-tan or black-and-gold Shepherds are probably the most popular, with all colors usually preferred to white. Color-related differences in temperament are minimal; vets and breeders consider all Shepherds to be equally trainable, with no color more prone to behavior such as protective or anxious barking, or whining for attention. Black Shepherds are generally regarded as the most relaxed, affable family companions — slightly more eager to be petted, less destructive when left alone, more playful with other dogs, and less likely to disobey. White Shepherds are usually reported to be the most nervous and disobedient, but the breed's overall character remains outstanding.

SABLE COAT
Black-tipped hairs denote a sable coat.

BLACK-AND-TAN SHORT COAT
This show champion female's well-defined, rich markings are a fine example of the classic black-and-tan German Shepherd coloration.

SABLE, LONG COAT
Lush, long coats such as this do not meet formal show standards, but their beauty is undeniable.

VARIETIES IN COAT LENGTH

Ninety percent of German Shepherds are born with standard short hair, and this is the length preferred by breeders. However, the richness and elegance of a long, feathery coat appeals to many Shepherd owners. Some dogs born with long hair have no undercoat, while others grow dense down, which offers excellent insulation but requires more frequent grooming. Short hair is relatively easy to care for, but long hair can become tangled and laden with debris or, in winter, pendulous blankets of snow.

BLACK-AND-GOLD
Deep gold tones give a warm accent to this dog's fluffy coat.

BLACK, LONG COAT
The luxurious coat of this all black Shepherd features many long, wispy tufts of hair.

BLACK-AND-TAN LONG COAT
Standard colors are attractively combined with a longer-style coat.

WHITE SHEPHERDS

White Shepherds are disqualified from the show ring in some countries and severely penalized in others. The spurious explanation given is that white working dogs are difficult to see on snow-covered hills, or too easy to spot as night-time guards. Hence, this color is bypassed by most top breeders and consequently disadvantaged. White Shepherds' unique look, however, gives them widespread popularity as pets.

WHITE, SHORT COAT
The almost pure white coloration makes for a striking appearance.

LONG COAT
Cream shades dominate here.

SEX AND TYPE DIFFERENCES

APART FROM THEIR OBVIOUS physical differences, male and female German Shepherds also vary somewhat in character. Specific "types" bred primarily for working or showing may differ too. Yet all have in common the alert, adaptable nature that has given the breed its well-earned popularity.

PHYSIQUE AND TEMPERAMENT: THE SEXES COMPARED

Male German Shepherds are typically larger and more powerfully built than females, and have less delicate features. Overall, gender also has some influence on personality, with male dogs being frequently more territorial and independently minded than females.

Head is narrower and smaller than male's

Body is less bulky and lighter, while retaining same proportions

GENTLE, RESPONSIVE FEMALE
Females are often regarded as slightly easier to train than males, and less disobedient. They are also more likely to be playful with other dogs and receptive to strangers, and may want more frequent petting than males. Neutering can sometimes reduce an inclination toward possessiveness.

GENDER-SPECIFIC MEDICAL PROBLEMS

A variety of diseases are caused or influenced by sex hormones. Unless spayed early in life, females of all breeds may suffer from breast cancer and womb infection. Uncastrated males sometimes develop anal tumors, testicular cancer, or prostate disorders, with associated pain or bleeding on urination. Neutering is part of the preferred treatment for all gender-related medical conditions. Subsequent weight gain is not a major problem with Shepherds.

ASSERTIVE, CONFIDENT MALE
Male Shepherds tend to be more territorial than females, and more wary of strangers, yet are generally not as excitable or as prone to whining for attention. Often more aloof and independent, they can require greater experience to train. Males of all breeds may instinctively try to dominate other male dogs.

Male has larger, heavier body and broader head than female

SHOW OR WORKING TYPE?

BRED FOR BEAUTY

Many Shepherds are bred to conform to the "type" that is favored in the show ring. "Type" is used to describe body proportions – the relationship between body length and shoulder height, and muzzle length and the size of the skull. Since this may be variously interpreted, show Shepherds have evolved over the years and continue to vary from country to country.

Successful show dog, trained in formal deportment, adopts presentation stance

Long, flowing top line curves gently downward to tail

Short coat length is considered correct for show ring

Working dog has been trained to retrieve dumbbell

Long coat is no disadvantage in an active role

TRAINED TO WORK

Some Shepherds bred for show are also trained to participate in working trials, which require skills in obedience, agility, or scent tracking. However, breeders who specialize in producing working "types" are inclined to select their stock from dogs that have excelled in these abilities. Performance potential is valued over perfect looks.

BREEDING FOR SPECIAL ROLES

German Shepherds destined for specific service duties such as police and security work, or assisting the disabled, are also selectively bred for certain desirable qualities. Sound health and good character are of prime importance, and dogs are screened for freedom from inherited physical disorders such as hip dysplasia and, even more importantly, for an even, calm temperament. In appearance, Shepherds with specialized jobs often depart from the type preferred in top show circles.

FINDING THE RIGHT DOG

HAVING DECIDED THAT you want to acquire a German Shepherd, be selective in your search. Do not act impulsively; seek professional guidance from your local vet or dog training club, and choose carefully according to this advice and your lifestyle. Any purchase should incorporate a veterinary examination.

ADVICE ON WHERE TO BUY AND WHAT TO LOOK FOR

CONSULT A VETERINARIAN
Vets and their staff can provide unbiased information on what to look for in a healthy German Shepherd. They are usually aware of any prevalent medical problems or behavioral idiosyncracies, and their advice is always free of charge.

INQUIRE AT LOCAL DOG TRAINING CLUBS
Contact your local dog training club for sound guidance on how to find a trainable, even-tempered Shepherd. Trainers are often able to recommend specific breeders. While gender and coat color partly determine a dog's temperament, so do breeding lines.

SUITABLE FOR YOUR LIFESTYLE?

It is important to select a dog that fits into your daily routine both now and as you foresee it in years to come. A German Shepherd is a large, active dog, needing plenty of exercise and mental stimulation. If you are new to the breed, ask other owners about their dogs and try to spend some time with one. If you have a family, acquiring a pet must be a collective decision. Make sure that all family members like the idea, and participate in your search for the right dog.

Pet German Shepherd is established as well-loved member of family

DECIDING ON A PUPPY OR AN ADULT DOG

BUYING A PUREBRED PUPPY

Although puppies are undoubtedly appealing, they are also very lively and demand lots of attention; be prepared! Reputable breeders, either professional or amateur, are the best source for German Shepherd puppies. Always visit several litters before making your choice, and note the physique and temperament of the mother and, if possible, the father too. Resist the temptation to buy the first puppy that catches your eye.

Puppies will be ready to leave the litter at about eight weeks

ANIMAL RESCUE CENTERS

Animal shelters always have dogs needing good homes. A rescued Shepherd from a traumatic background is naturally more likely to have behavior problems, notably anxiety when left alone. Such dogs may take some time to settle into a new home, but can make exceedingly devoted and affectionate companions. An adult dog from a rescue center could be a sound option if you feel daunted by the prospect of an energetic puppy and want to avoid the inconvenience of house training. However, because unexpected personality quirks can often be difficult to deal with, only experienced dog owners should acquire "recycled" German Shepherds.

HEALTH CHECKS FOR YOUR NEW DOG

Ears are inspected as part of thorough examination

Make any purchase conditional upon your vet's confirmation that the dog is healthy, with no sign of infectious disease, malnutrition, or parasites. Breeders should provide documents verifying that a puppy's parents are free from a variety of hereditary disorders. By law, if a puppy is not healthy at sale, you are entitled to a refund or a replacement.

AVOID PUPPY MILLS

Whenever possible, purchase your dog directly from a breeder. Avoid puppy farms or mills, as they often provide inhumane environments for mothers and give little attention to the puppies' health. Newspaper advertisements can be fronts for mills; be suspicious if when visiting a private home you cannot see the litter's mother. Be wary also of pet shops; some buy from puppy mills and can be fertile environments for a variety of infectious diseases.

YOUR NEW PUPPY

IDEALLY, BUY YOUR GERMAN SHEPHERD puppy from a recommended breeder when it is about eight weeks old. Older puppies and young adults may find it harder adapting to a new home. Make a careful choice after viewing several litters, then get everything ready to help ensure a smooth introduction for all.

CHOOSING THE RIGHT PUPPY

VISITING A LITTER

When viewing a litter, watch how the puppies behave together; some may be retiring, others more bossy. Bear in mind that very assertive puppies often develop into dominant adults and can be more difficult to train, while a shy puppy may grow to be insecure or fearful – a fairly common occurrence in Shepherds. Apart from considering temperament, decide which sex you prefer, then select a puppy that seems bright, alert, and healthy.

Healthy puppy feels firm, and surprisingly heavy

Easy-going puppy is relaxed and content to be handled

THE ONE FOR YOU?

When picking up or holding a very young puppy, always support its hindquarters. If you are new to Shepherds, do not choose the most forward and confident puppy; this one will need experienced handling. Pick the average of the litter, neither too bold nor overly submissive. Ask to see the parents' registration documents, and health certificates verifying that they are free from hereditary conditions common to the breed, such as hip dysplasia.

MEET THE PARENTS

Responsible breeders are proud of their stock and will be delighted to introduce you to the litter's mother and also the father if available. The parents' appearance and behavior will give some idea of your puppy's mature size and likely temperament. Be cautious with individuals who are unable to show you the mother; they may not be genuine breeders but agents for puppy mills. Reputable breeders will also allow you to return a puppy immediately if your vet feels there is good reason to do so.

SETTLING IN AT HOME

Secure crate allows gentle exposure to new environment

GETTING ACQUAINTED

As soon as you arrive home with your new puppy, introduce it to its own secure "den" – a grilled dog crate lined with soft bedding is ideal. Initially, make the crate inviting by placing food treats or toys inside, and leave the door open. When the door is shut, a resident dog is able to investigate without fear of harassment.

FIRST NIGHT ALONE

The first night that your puppy is away from its brothers and sisters and in new surroundings is always the most difficult. Provide it with a chewable toy for comfort and, if you are willing, place the crate in your bedroom so the puppy is reassured by your presence. Do not respond to plaintive cries, however, or you will unwittingly train your puppy to whine for attention.

Puppy may be restless or anxious at first

SWEET DREAMS

With a little perseverance, your puppy will learn to settle down and sleep. Set your alarm so that you can get up during the night for the first few weeks to take your puppy to relieve itself. Alternatively, line one side of the crate with bedding and the other with paper for soiling. When your puppy is a bit older, it should accept sleeping outside of your bedroom.

EARLY TRAINING

AFTER YOUR PUPPY has settled in to its new home, begin gentle training for obedience and hygiene. Reward good behavior with praise, stroking, or food treats. Provide toys to keep your puppy alert and occupied, and arrange regular contact with other dogs to ensure proper social development.

LEARNING WITH REWARDS

VERBAL PRAISE

Shepherds are eager pupils and learn quickly. Even a very young puppy will be sensitive to your manner and tone of voice, and will understand when you are genuinely pleased with its behavior. Enthusiastic words of approval should always accompany any other type of reward.

Touching the head can be seen as a threat; stroke the body instead

Puppy knows it has done well when it hears "Good dog!"

STROKING REWARD

Touch is an intensely powerful reward. Your puppy will naturally want to be stroked, but do not comply on demand. Offer petting in response to good conduct, so that obedience is associated with desired physical attention.

ACQUIRING SOCIAL SKILLS

A puppy's ability to learn is at its greatest during the first three months. If denied ongoing contact with other dogs during this important stage, your German Shepherd may not develop the social skills necessary for meeting strange dogs later in life. If you do not have another dog, ask your vet to help you organize regular supervised "puppy parties" to encourage natural, friendly interaction between healthy puppies of a similar age.

Favorite foods are useful as rewards for good behavior

FOOD TREAT

Some German Shepherds are so alert to their surroundings that they do not respond immediately to food rewards. Discover which treats your puppy likes best and use these as rewards, along with vigorous praise.

TOYS FOR YOUR NEW PUPPY

Chew toy is excellent for exercising puppy's jaw muscles

SUITABLE TOYS FOR CHEWING AND PLAYING
Well-designed toys help stimulate your puppy physically and mentally. However, Shepherds can be possessive about toys – particularly squeaky ones. Therefore, let your dog see you put all play items away after use, so it understands that they belong to you. Keep only a limited collection of toys, choosing ones that are fun to chase, capture, retrieve, or chew.

TOYS AS REWARD AND COMFORT
While toys left lying around soon become boring, items brought out only under special circumstances are transformed into exciting rewards. When given selectively as a prize for good behavior, toys can serve as extremely effective training aids. Whenever you leave your Shepherd alone, at any age, be sure to provide it with a well-loved toy as comforting distraction.

HOUSE TRAINING INDOORS AND OUT

PAPER TRAINING
Your puppy will usually want to eliminate after waking, eating, drinking, or exercise. It may signal this by putting its nose down and sniffing. Quickly place the dog in an area covered with newspaper, and praise it when it urinates or defecates. It is pointless to punish your puppy after an accident. If you catch it in the act, however, sternly say "No" to teach it that it must use the paper.

MOVING OUTSIDE
Start outdoor training as soon as possible. Three-month-old puppies need to empty their bladders about every three hours. Take a small piece of soiled paper with you; the puppy will smell its own scent and be encouraged to transfer toileting outside. As it eliminates, say "Hurry up"; this will train your dog to relieve itself on that command.

INTRODUCING OUTDOORS

PUPPIES SHOULD EXPERIENCE the outdoors as soon as possible. Provide essential health vaccinations and identification, and accustom your young Shepherd to a collar and lead. Enlist friends to help you create situations in which the puppy can meet new people and other dogs in controlled circumstances.

IDENTIFICATION

STANDARD NAME TAG
Engraved or canister tags carry vital information about your dog, including a contact telephone number. A dab of nail varnish will keep metal canisters from unscrewing.

MICROCHIP
A tiny microchip, encased in glass, stores important data permanently. Inserted just under the skin on the neck, it can be "read" using a hand-held scanner.

EAR TATTOO
Painless tattoos, bearing a registration number logged with a kennel club or other private organization, provide permanent identification and are widely popular.

INTRODUCTION TO COLLAR AND LEAD

1 Collar and lead training can begin as soon as you acquire your puppy. Start by letting the dog see and smell the collar. Then, avoiding eye contact, kneel down and put the collar on, distracting the puppy with words. Reward it with treats, physical contact, and praise. Actively play for a while, then take the collar off. Your puppy will quickly learn to associate the collar with rewards, and should accept it without reluctance.

Put on a light, comfortable collar, distracting puppy with words, or using a treat or toy

2 Once your puppy is content wearing its collar, kneel in front and attach a lead. Keeping the lead slack, entice your dog to one side with a toy or food reward. When it moves toward the reward, apply light tension to the lead. Allow the puppy to have the toy or treat, and give it copious praise.

Puppy is rewarded for accepting presence and light tension of lead by gaining access to toy

MEETING STRANGERS

Arrange for a canine-loving friend to meet you and your dog outdoors. Ask your friend to kneel down to greet the puppy, as this will help dissuade it from jumping up. Also discourage direct eye contact, which can provoke a fearful or nervous response – not uncommon in Shepherds. Finally, provide your friend with your puppy's favorite food treat to give as a reward for calmness.

Prevent jumping by kneeling rather than leaning over puppy

ESSENTIAL PUPPY INOCULATIONS

Your vet will vaccinate your new puppy against a range of infectious diseases, and for extra protection may advise avoidance of unfamiliar dogs for a few weeks. Contact with known healthy dogs should continue, however, to ensure proper socialization.

ENCOUNTERING OTHER DOGS

Ask a friend with a relaxed dog to meet you on a walk. Have your friend instruct her dog to sit while you walk past, and reward your puppy's calm response with treats and praise. If you have no friends with dogs, you will find that other dog walkers are more than willing to help with this form of training. Through routine meetings, your puppy learns that there is no need to be fearful of other dogs. Regular interaction with puppies of a similar age will also help in developing vital social skills.

Always walk your puppy on a lead for safe control

Well-behaved adult dog sits placidly on command without provoking puppy

Puppy shows interest in strange dog but no anxiety

FIRST ROUTINES

A PUPPY'S EARLY EXPERIENCES set patterns for life. Train your young Shepherd from its first days with you to accept being left alone, to wait patiently in its own crate while you are busy, and to learn about permitted behavior. Most importantly, train it to enjoy coming to you when called.

ACCEPTING BEING LEFT ALONE

No matter how much you enjoy being with your new puppy, there will be times when you must leave it on its own. Train your young Shepherd to accept that this is part of its routine by confining it to its crate with an interesting reward, such as a hollow toy filled with a little peanut butter. Then quietly walk away, signaling "Wait." Gradually accustom your dog to being left alone for extended periods.

Puppy is content in crate because it has been rewarded with favorite toy

Owner quietly walks away, giving hand signal that puppy will soon learn means "Wait"

DISTINGUISHING BETWEEN GOOD AND BAD BEHAVIOR

Without training, your puppy will simply follow its own natural instincts. Behavior expectations must be taught, by rewarding good conduct and reprimanding disagreeable actions. Shepherds are very sensitive to tone of voice, and a stern "No!" is powerful admonition. To punish substantial misdemeanors, you may grab the scruff of the neck firmly but without causing pain, mimicking how the puppy's mother would have administered discipline.

SEVERAL PUPPIES?

If you have more than one puppy, train them individually for effective results. It is very difficult, even for highly experienced dog handlers, to maintain the concentration of several lively puppies together!

COMING TO YOU ON COMMAND

1 For safety and responsible control, your puppy must learn always to come to you on command. Use positive training with rewards; never call your puppy to discipline it, or it will then associate returning to you with being reprimanded. Having trained your Shepherd to accept a collar and lead, put these on the dog and kneel a short distance away, with the lead tucked securely under one knee. Hold a chewable or attractively scented toy as a reward; this will be more clearly visible than a food treat.

Appealing toy makes training fun for your dog

Puppies are easily distracted and may ignore you initially

2 Call your puppy's name in a clear, friendly tone to attract its attention. When it turns its head toward you, give the command "Come" and wave the toy as an enticement. Keep the lead slack; do not reel in your puppy but encourage it to come willingly for the reward.

When called, puppy turns and sees toy

Tail held high shows puppy is now alert and eager to obey

3 Welcome your puppy with open arms. Out of curiosity, it should walk toward you. As it moves, say "Good dog" in an enthusiastic voice. When the puppy reaches you, reward it with the toy. Develop a pleasurable bond so your dog comes because it wants to be with you.

COME, SIT, DOWN, STAY

TRAINING YOUR PUPPY to come, sit, lie down, and stay down is most important both for the safety of your dog and for harmonious relations with your family, friends, and outside the home. As a breed, the German Shepherd is exceptionally responsive to basic obedience training.

COME AND SIT

While training, maintain eye contact with your puppy

1 Try to work in a quiet, narrow space such as a hallway, without any distractions. Holding the puppy on a loose lead, cheerfully call its name and let it see that you have a food treat in your hand. As it begins to move, give the command "Come." Be enthusiastic, and while your puppy walks toward you, praise it by saying "Good dog."

Lead is slack, but can be gently pulled to gain compliance

2 When your puppy reaches you, move the treat above its head. To keep its eye on the food, the puppy will naturally sit. As it does so, issue the command "Sit" and immediately give the reward. Repeat the exercise regularly until your puppy responds to words alone.

Offer reward calmly to avoid over-excitement

Tail held out shows puppy is not anxious or frightened

THE UNRESPONSIVE PUPPY

Some German Shepherds are simply not interested in food rewards. While training your puppy, feed it fewer but larger meals to stimulate the appetite. If this fails, try using a favorite squeaky toy as a reward. Puppies can also be easily distracted, so begin basic training in a quiet indoor environment before moving outside, where there are more diversions for a lively and curious dog. Train only for a few minutes at a time twice daily when you, as well as your puppy, are mentally alert. With a strong-willed puppy, use a lead to ensure that it responds.

Puppy stretches along floor to receive food treat

SIT AND DOWN

1 Kneel beside the seated puppy, holding its collar with one hand, and place a treat by its nose. If your puppy will not sit or tries to get up, tuck its hindquarters under with your free hand and command "Sit."

2 Move the treat forward and down in an arc, drawing the puppy as it follows the food with its nose. As it starts to lie down, give the command "Down." If the puppy refuses, gently raise its front legs into a begging position, then lower it down, always rewarding obedience with praise.

Lead is secured under knee to maintain control

3 Still holding the collar, continue to move the treat forward and down until your puppy is lying completely flat. Then reward the puppy with the treat and praise. Do not praise excessively, however; this can excite your young Shepherd and be counter-productive.

STAY DOWN

Having positioned your puppy down, give the command "Stay." With the lead held loosely in your hand, and maintaining eye contact, get up and walk in front, repeating "Stay." Use a raised palm gesture rather than food rewards; this will become a learned visual signal. Response to the "Stay" command is important in potentially hazardous situations.

Gradually extend length of "Stay" to minutes

TRAINING TO HEEL

A MATURE GERMAN SHEPHERD running loose or pulling on its lead can be intimidating to some people, while a mild-mannered Shepherd walking to heel is the perfect advertisement for such a marvelous breed. Some puppies initially train best for heelwork off the lead; others respond well to a lead from the start.

TRAINING TO HEEL WITHOUT A LEAD

1 Kneel to the right of your alert, seated puppy. Holding its collar with your left hand, speak its name and show it a food treat in your other hand.

2 Using the scent of the food to attract the puppy, walk in a straight line while giving the command "Heel." Be ready to grasp the collar with your left hand if the puppy wanders. When you stop, command "Wait." Have your dog master the sequence of "Sit," "Heel," and "Wait" before progressing to right and left turns.

Puppy eagerly follows food; or, try a favorite toy

3 Keeping the treat low to prevent jumping up, bend your knees and turn right, drawing the food around as you move. Repeat the command "Heel." Your puppy will speed up to walk around you.

Train puppy to stay close to your leg

4 Left turns are more difficult. Hold the collar with your left hand and give the command "Steady." Place the reward close to your dog's mouth, then move it to the left. The puppy will follow.

Puppy turns to left in pursuit of reward

Heelwork with a Lead

1 With the puppy on a long training lead and seated to your left, hold the lead and a treat in your right hand, and the slack of the lead in your left. Tell your puppy to sit.

Puppy watches owner intently

Maintain eye contact as puppy waits for next command

2 Move forward on your left foot while giving the command "Heel." If your puppy strays too far ahead, give the lead a quick, light jerk to pull it back.

3 With the puppy beside you in the heel position, offer it the reward and say "Good dog." Repeat the "Sit" command, and praise your puppy when it obeys.

5 Once the right turn has been learned, begin left-turn training. Hold the treat in front of the puppy's nose to slow it down while speeding up your own circling movement to the left. Keep the puppy close to your left leg and issue the command "Steady" as it follows you around.

4 After the dog has learned to walk to heel in a straight line, teach it to turn to the right by guiding it with the treat. If your puppy has lost interest, break off practice until later.

Puppy slows down while concentrating on food reward

INDOOR TRAINING

ALTHOUGH GERMAN SHEPHERDS love the outdoors, your dog is likely to spend much of its life with you in your home. Make sure that it understands basic "house rules," and provide it with its own personal space and bed. Give your Shepherd satisfying time and attention, but always on your own terms.

LEARNING TO WAIT PATIENTLY

Your German Shepherd must be made to understand that you are the leader of the pack, and you decide what happens and when. Do not respond to your dog's demands for attention or let it initiate activities. Every dog should have some private space – a bed or a crate that it can call its own. Your Shepherd will learn to retire happily to its "den" while you are relaxing or busy with household chores.

Quilt-type bed is comfortable and large enough for adult dog to stretch out fully

Dog chews toy, not disturbing owner

SPENDING QUALITY TIME TOGETHER

Nurturing the bond between you and your dog is not only enjoyable, but important in reinforcing basic obedience. Set aside time each day to offer your Shepherd some indoor physical and mental activity. Vary the hour and type of play, or your dog will expect a certain game at a given time. Put toys away at the end of play; this makes their next appearance more exciting.

Games keep your dog happy and alert, and are rewarding for both players

Understanding What Is Wrong

Use body language as well as words to convey your displeasure

No dog instinctively knows what is permitted and what is not. For example, lying on a comfortable sofa seems perfectly natural to your Shepherd! Unwanted behavior should be reprimanded immediately so the dog understands exactly what it has done wrong. Be theatrical, adopting an assertive stance and a stern tone of voice, and your dog will quickly learn your intentions.

Relinquishing a Forbidden Item

Female Shepherds are particularly likely to appropriate appealing objects and take them back to their beds, although males may also smuggle food-scented items like kitchen cloths. Train your dog, using favorite treats, to drop and surrender forbidden articles willingly on command.

Accepting Strangers at Home

German Shepherds are inclined to bark protectively and "patrol" the home. Some may even try to dominate visitors by jumping up or growling. Train your dog to sit calmly at a distance when guests are present, to discourage territorial guarding. Ask visitors initially to disregard your pet and avoid eye contact; this will help disperse any sense of confrontation. If your Shepherd is vocal, teach it to be quiet on command. Always reward good behavior with approving words, a gentle stroke, or a favorite treat.

OUTSIDE THE HOME

WHETHER IN YOUR OWN YARD or farther afield, your German Shepherd must be kept under secure control, both for its own protection and the safety of others. It is important to provide a healthy, hazard-free environment for your pet, and to observe social obligations conscientiously.

SHELTER AND EXERCISE

COMFORTABLE OUTDOOR KENNEL
If you plan to house your dog in a kennel, introduce it at an early age. The kennel should be chew-proof and well-insulated. Make it a cozy sanctuary, but do not keep your dog kenneled alone interminably.

CLEAN, SPACIOUS RUN
A hygienic run attached to the kennel is ideal for several dogs, allowing fresh air and limited exercise. However, Shepherds have large reserves of energy and will still need regular physical activity outside their runs.

CONTROL OUTDOORS

HUMANE CHOKE COLLAR
Most dogs respond well to a humane choke collar. Fit it so that the soft webbing lies around your dog's throat, while the chain links sit at the back of its neck. A tug on the lead will tighten the collar, giving firm control without causing discomfort.

HEAD HALTER
A head halter can help with strong-willed dogs. Ensure that it fits comfortably over the muzzle. If your Shepherd lunges, its momentum will gently tighten the nylon halter, pulling the head down and the jaws closed.

MUZZLE
Apply a muzzle either to obey local laws or to prevent your dog from biting. Use a basket variety in the appropriate size and properly adjusted to permit panting and barking. Never leave your muzzled dog unattended for long periods.

Using a Choke Chain

1 To put on a choke chain correctly, hold it open as shown, then slip it around your dog's neck.

2 The chain must tighten only when tension is applied to the lead. If put on backward, or if the dog is not kept on your left side, the chain will not loosen after tension is released.

Always Give Prompt Discipline

German Shepherds are lively, inquisitive dogs that, left unsupervised, may investigate further than you would like. If your dog has engaged in destructive digging, for example, reprimand it at once so it understands why you are displeased. Command it to lie down and stop play; if you are away from home, return immediately. Young male Shepherds in particular may need obedience reinforced when outdoors.

Planning a Safe and Secure Yard

The greatest hazard presented by your yard is the risk of escape. Check that all fencing is sturdy, gate latches secure, and that hedges have no gaps. Install wire mesh where necessary. Keep all garden chemicals safely locked away, and if you have outdoor lighting, ensure that no cables are exposed and may be chewed. To prevent damage to your lawn, train your dog to use a specific site as its toilet. Be certain to store all garbage and any horticultural tools securely out of reach, and do not plant material that may be poisonous to dogs. Always watch your Shepherd carefully near a lit barbecue so it does not lick hot implements, and cover ornamental ponds to avoid accidents.

Housing for garbage cans

Wire mesh beneath locked gate

Sturdy fencing

Rotting compost contained in bin

Greenhouse stores garden chemicals

Sand-pit toilet

Non-toxic plants

Fenced-in vegetable garden

Plant pots tied together for stability

Covered pond

Lit barbecue must be supervised

Enclosed dog house

TRAVEL AND BOARDING

WITH PROPER CARE, your Shepherd should happily accept both routine travel and vacations. Introduce car journeys as early as possible, and make trips safe and enjoyable. Monitor your dog in any new surroundings, and ensure that it will be secure and comfortable if left with others while you are away.

QUALITY BOARDING KENNELS

For vacations without your dog, ask your vet's advice on kennels. Visit recommended establishments and inspect their housing and runs for cleanliness and security. Ask how often your Shepherd will be exercised or played with each day, and satisfy yourself that the staff are responsible. If introduced to kennels early in life, dogs tend to take revisits in stride. Before kenneling, ensure that your dog's health inoculations are up to date.

DOG-SITTING SERVICES

Especially in urban areas, dog- and house-sitting services are an alternative to kennels. Again, your vet may be able to recommend reliable agencies providing Shepherd-loving carers to look after your home and your dog while you are away. Always leave dog sitters with a list of routine instructions, emergency details, and house rules for your dog.

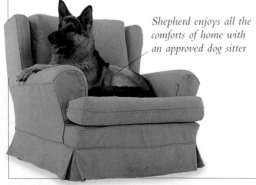

Shepherd enjoys all the comforts of home with an approved dog sitter

BE CONSIDERATE OF OTHERS

Local dog-control regulations vary. Observe notices, and keep your dog on a lead and under control where obliged. Carry a supply of plastic bags to clean up after your dog, and deposit mess in special trash cans if available. Never let your dog be a nuisance to others.

SAFE TRAVELING BY CAR

REAR-LOADED CRATE
Professional dog handlers prefer to transport
their dogs in crates. Roomy and secure, they
help keep your car free from dog hair or chewing
damage. Introduce your Shepherd to its crate
during puppyhood, as its regular bed and playpen.
Then, when the crate is used as transportation, it
will be inclined to relax and enjoy the journey.
On long trips, stop periodically to allow your
dog to exercise, drink, and relieve itself.

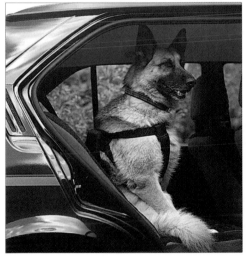

CANINE SEATBELT
Your Shepherd risks the same injuries that you
do in a car accident. Your dog can travel safely
on the rear seat of a car using a special canine
seatbelt which, like a child's harness, attaches to
the standard seatbelt anchors. With this, the dog
is kept reassuringly in place and under control,
so that it cannot distract the driver. Alternatively,
restrict your dog to the back of a van or station
wagon equipped with a sturdy dog grille.

DEFENDING TERRITORY

Shepherds are territorial, and a car makes a natural "den"
to defend. Your dog's presence is usually enough to deter
intruders, but it may still growl or snap at
passers-by. If your dog shows such
aggression or persistently barks at
activity outside, install sunblinds
as screening, or sit with it for
retraining, admonishing bad
behavior. Remember, never
leave your dog car-bound in
hot or sunny weather – even
with the windows slightly open –
or with the heater on in winter, as
the Shepherd's typically dark coat makes it
particularly susceptible to potentially fatal heatstroke.

CONSTRUCTIVE PLAY

GERMAN SHEPHERDS NEED a great deal of physical exercise, but adequate mental stimulation is equally vital. Create activities that make the most of the breed's resourcefulness and superb trainability. Use playtime to reinforce basic training, to strengthen your bond as owner, and simply to have fun.

RETRIEVE ON COMMAND

Although the German Shepherd is not selectively bred for retrieving, your dog can easily be taught to fetch any item. With praise, train it to hold an object such as a slipper, and then to pick the object up. Progress by teaching the command "Fetch," sending your dog away to retrieve the item, followed by "Come." Ensure a response initially by using a lead, and make sure your dog knows exactly what you want it to retrieve.

"SPEAK" AND "HUSH"

Pre-empt barking problems by training your dog, using food or toy rewards, to "Speak" on command. Once it has mastered barking to order, your Shepherd is ready to learn to be quiet when it hears the word "Hush." This useful "game" helps to enforce household peace while allowing watchdog barking to be turned on and off on your direction.

LEARNED ROUTINES

Physical games are the most exciting for your dog, but even "playing dead" can be enjoyable when rewarded with treats, active play, or praise. This entertaining routine is an extension of the "Down" command, with your Shepherd learning to lie still until you release it by saying "OK."

Dog obligingly collapses at signal "Bang"

EAGER TO WORK

Satisfy your Shepherd's innate curiosity and desire to serve by giving it something to do. Carrying a newspaper or even a light load of shopping is a pleasant challenge, and your dog will relish the opportunity to assist. Helpful behavior should always be heartily rewarded.

Giving paw shows dog recognizes your authority

TOYS BELONG TO YOU

When you finish playing, make a point of collecting and putting away all toys. This re-establishes that you are in charge, and playtime is available only through you. It also makes toys more desirable to your dog, and therefore more useful to you as a control tool. Some German Shepherds are possessive, and should be trained to relinquish toys in exchange for treats, lavish praise, or other favorite rewards.

Toy is surrendered for food reward

GAME OF "HIGH FIVE"

Giving a paw is a submissive gesture. Training your Shepherd to sit and offer its paw helps reinforce that you are the natural leader. When children play "High Five" with the dog, it learns that they too are in command.

THE OWNER ALWAYS WINS

Forget about democracy when playing with your Shepherd. It may see certain games as a challenge rather than simple fun, and must be made to understand that you are always the victor. Avoid activities that are too stimulating, like tug-of-war; your dog might want to win so much that it forgets some of its training.

Ensure that play is still satisfying by finishing all games on a positive note, with food rewards, stroking, or encouraging words.

Store play items in toybox to control game time

GOOD CONTROL

LIKE ALL OTHER DOGS, your German Shepherd may present you with behavior problems. Some Shepherds are sensitive to the unfamiliar; others may be troublesomely curious. Most difficulties can be prevented or overcome through proper care and training, and by establishing positive control.

Dog chews toy contentedly while owner is away

HAPPILY OCCUPIED ALONE

No dog enjoys being left alone, and separation anxiety or boredom can result in destructive behavior. Always leave and return without a fuss, and exercise and feed your dog before you go out, to encourage rest. Give it a favorite toy, or one with a hollow center that you have filled with cheese spread or peanut butter.

ACCEPTING UNFAMILIAR SITUATIONS

If your dog is alarmed by a new sight or sound, re-present the stimulus from a distance that does not provoke distress. Reward composure with treats and gentle words. Over several weeks, bring the disturbing object gradually nearer, always rewarding calm acceptance. Your dog will follow your lead and see that there is no cause for concern.

Dog is wary of child on skateboard

Relaxed, easy-going Labrador is used as the "stooge"

Lead ensures control for first meeting

FRIENDLINESS WITH OTHER DOGS

A well-socialized dog will show curious interest rather than apprehension or hostility when meeting other dogs. If your Shepherd is fearful or aggressive, introduce it to a placid, even-tempered dog. Find a distance where your dog is at ease, and give it a reward. Over time, draw the two dogs closer together. Reward good behavior on each occasion, teaching your Shepherd not to regard other dogs as a threat.

Dog sits politely, accepting presence of stranger

MEETING STRANGERS

If your Shepherd greets strangers with protective aggression, ask fellow dog-lovers to help in practice meetings. Have them avoid potentially intimidating eye contact with your pet, command your dog to sit, and give rewards when it shows no antagonism. Ask a friend to offer a food treat or toy so your dog learns to welcome approaches from new people. Always stop exercise or games if your Shepherd acts aggressively.

DEALING WITH A WILFUL DOG

Some German Shepherds are more dominant than others and need firm handling. If your dog does not respond to your commands, withdraw all rewards – and that includes your affection! Do not take risks; if you are inexperienced with dogs or concerned about your Shepherd's behavior, contact your vet or local training club and arrange one-to-one or group obedience lessons. Remember, one ill-mannered Shepherd tarnishes the reputation of the entire breed.

LEARNING TO IGNORE DISTRACTIONS

Owner jerks lead to enforce verbal command "Come"

Even the most obedient Shepherd may lapse when faced with a tantalizing diversion. After training your dog to come on command, create an enticing distraction such as a succulent bone. Recall your dog, using an extendible lead to enforce your command. Trained in this way, your dog will learn to return to you on most, if not all, occasions!

Use extendible lead until dog responds willingly

While investigating bone, dog becomes "deaf" to instruction

RESISTING TEMPTATION

Prevent begging by never giving food while you are eating. Relenting with the occasional titbit will actually encourage this bad behavior more than regular offerings. If your dog begs, command it to lie down, then look away. When you have finished eating, reward your Shepherd's obedience with play and approving words, not with food treats.

Child avoids eye contact while eating ice-cream

FOODS FOR YOUR DOG

CONSIDERING THEIR SIZE and energy demands, Shepherds can be surprisingly choosy eaters. Fortunately, there is a vast array of commercially prepared and home-cooked foods to meet both nutritional needs and personal tastes. Remember that you are in control of what your dog eats, not the dog.

CANNED FOODS

Moist, meaty canned foods come in a wide range of flavors and textures to suit your Shepherd's appetite. High in protein, they are usually mixed with dry dog meal to add calories and vital carbohydrates. Canned foods are nutritious and tasty, but will not stay fresh in the bowl for more than a few hours.

Standard variety

Special formula for clinical conditions

"Stew" with gravy

Chunks in jelly

DRY MEAL

Crunchy dry meal is added to canned food to improve the texture, contribute fiber and fat, as well as exercise the jaws.

COMPLETE DRY FOODS

Complete dry foods are well-balanced and convenient to store in bulk. Concentrated, they contain about four times the calories of canned foods, so a dog needs smaller quantities. There are varieties to suit all ages and for specific needs, including medical conditions such as bowel inflammation, to which Shepherds can be susceptible.

HIGH-ENERGY
Puppies require nutrient-rich, easily digestible foods to sustain growth.

REGULAR
Adult formulas maintain mature dogs on a variety of activity levels.

LOW-CALORIE
Older, overweight, or sedentary dogs need less energy from their food.

TEETH-CLEANING
These large, crunchy chunks promote healthy gums and help control tartar.

SEMIMOIST FOODS

These foods are packaged in many flavors, including cheese, and have three times the calories of canned foods. A high carbohydrate content makes semimoist foods unsuitable for diabetic dogs. Like dry foods, they can be left out all day, allowing a picky or elderly Shepherd to nibble at its own pace.

SUITABLE CHEWS

Dogs need hard chews to work their teeth. Avoid small chews that may be swallowed, or bones which can fracture teeth.

Compressed biscuit chew

TREATS AND BISCUITS

Snack foods can be very useful training aids. Discover which treats your dog likes best, and give these as rewards for good behavior, not on demand. Although obesity is not a serious problem with most Shepherds, limit the amount of high-calorie snacks given daily.

BACON-FLAVORED   SAVORY RINGS   MEATY CHUNKS   LIVER ROUNDS

TABLE FOODS

In general, a diet that is well-balanced for us is also nourishing for canines. Never encourage begging by feeding scraps from the table, but prepare a special portion for your dog. White meat with pasta or rice is an excellent meal, but avoid strong spices.

Chicken is easily digested and lower in calories than red meat

When serving, mix rice or pasta with meat to ensure all is eaten

CONVALESCING DIETS

German Shepherds are somewhat prone to gastrointestinal upsets. If your dog is recovering from illness, offer it easily digested foods such as scrambled eggs or a special diet prescribed by your vet.

Light, fresh-cooked scrambled eggs are ideal for sensitive stomachs

HEALTHY EATING

A NUTRITIOUS DIET and sound eating habits are essential to good health. Provide the right foods in the correct quantity for your dog's needs. Although German Shepherds are not generally as food-orientated as many other breeds, prevent begging or obesity by feeding at set times.

DIETARY NEEDS FOR ALL AGES

Puppy lies down for a relaxing meal

GROWING PUPPY
Puppies need plenty of nutrients for healthy growth. Up to 12 weeks of age, feed your puppy four times daily. Reduce this to three meals until it is six months old, then feed twice a day through to the first year.

Bowl has non-slip bottom for easier eating

FEEDING ROUTINES

It is important to establish a strict routine for mealtimes. Train your dog to sit and wait in the presence of food and to eat only when released to do so. Never offer tidbits while you are eating, and always give food in the dog's own bowl. Prevent food guarding in a puppy by touching it occasionally during its meals.

Dog waits patiently for signal to eat

MATURE ADULT
The dietary requirements of an adult dog vary enormously, depending upon its health, activity levels, and temperament. Relaxed, easy-going Shepherds may be prone to weight gain. As a general rule, feed your dog once or twice daily.

ELDERLY SHEPHERD
Older, as well as neutered, dogs have lower energy demands and should be fed smaller portions or less calorie-rich foods. Protein intake may be reduced to help prevent obesity, which places undue strain on the hind legs and organs such as the kidneys.

DAILY ENERGY DEMANDS FOR ALL STAGES OF LIFE

AGE	WEIGHT	CALORIES	DRY FOOD	SEMIMOIST	CANNED/MEAL
2 MONTHS	11 lb (4.5 kg)	1,005	11 oz (300 g)	12 oz (335 g)	18 oz/6 oz (500 g/170 g)
3 MONTHS	20 lb (9 kg)	1,560	16 oz (465 g)	18 oz (500 g)	28 oz/9 oz (780 g/265 g)
6 MONTHS	49 lb (22 kg)	2,160	23 oz (645 g)	25 oz (700 g)	38 oz/13 oz (1080 g/380 g)
TYPICAL ADULT	49–95 lb (22–43 kg)	1,120–1,850	12–20 oz (335–555 g)	13–22 oz (380–630 g)	20–33 oz/7–11 oz (555–925 g/190–300 g)
ACTIVE ADULT	49–95 lb (22–43 kg)	1,270–2,100	13–22 oz (380–630 g)	15–25 oz (425–700 g)	22–37 oz/8–13 oz (630–1050 g/215–380 g)
VERY ACTIVE ADULT	49–95 lb (22–43 kg)	1,780–2,940	19–31 oz (530–880 g)	21–35 oz (595–980 g)	31–52 oz/11–18 oz (880–1470 g/300–500 g)
ELDERLY (10 YEARS+)	49–95 lb (22–43 kg)	1,020–1,680	11–18 oz (300–500 g)	12–20 oz (335–555 g)	18–30 oz/6–10 oz (500–840 g/170–285 g)

FEEDING REQUIREMENTS

These figures represent an approximate guide only. Remember that each dog has its own specific nutritional needs, and that different brands of food vary in calories.

Always provide a well-balanced diet to meet your dog's energy requirements. If you are uncertain of what is best for your Shepherd, ask your vet for detailed advice.

THE RELUCTANT EATER

Unlike some breeds that will eat almost anything, Shepherds have a tendency to be fussy with food. If you and your vet are happy that your finicky dog is healthy and its meals nutritious and tasty, offer food for an hour and, if left untouched, take it away. Repeat this procedure daily until eating resumes. It may take several days, but hunger will eventually prevail over any fussy eater! Always provide plenty of fresh water to prevent life-threatening dehydration, particularly if your dog is receiving dry food.

Serve food at room temperature, never straight from the refrigerator

RED MEAT AND AGGRESSIVE BEHAVIOR

Regular high-protein meals may be related to forms of aggression. An unvarying diet of fresh meat, or cat food, is too rich and will supply more energy than a domestic Shepherd needs, potentially leading to excessively dominant behavior. If this is a concern, include plenty of carbohydrates and vegetables, or perhaps experiment with meat substitutes such as soy or tofu.

BASIC BODY CARE

GERMAN SHEPHERDS have a fine anatomy and are relatively easy to keep clean. Nevertheless, routine attention is required to keep your dog in good health. Examine its eyes, ears, and mouth daily, and brush the teeth every week. Shepherds' nails also tend to grow quickly and need regular clipping.

ENSURING CLEAR, HEALTHY EYES

Dampen cotton wool with tepid salt water to avoid loose fibers

The eyes should be bright, clear, and free from any discharge, inflammation, or cloudiness. Remove mucus or debris from the area surrounding the eye using a fresh, moistened cotton ball. Yellow or green discharge often indicates an infection and requires medical treatment. Also seek veterinary advice if your dog has watery eyes or blinks excessively.

BRUSHING THE TEETH

Check daily for any items lodged in the mouth or between the teeth. Once a week, clean the teeth with a soft brush, working up and down to massage the gums. Avoid human toothpaste, which froths and is swallowed.

PREVENT TOOTH TARTAR

Without routine cleaning, tartar can accumulate on the teeth, leading to bad breath, root infection, and gum disease. In addition to regular professional scaling and polishing, rawhide chews are helpful in controlling tartar build-up. This Shepherd's teeth and gums require medical attention.

INSPECTING THE EARS

When cleaning the ears, check for wax, inflammation, odor, crusty or scaly deposits, and foreign objects such as grass. Never probe too deeply, as wax can be pushed farther in.

Dull pink skin shows no discharge or wax

CUTTING THE NAILS

Command your dog to sit. Use a guillotine clipper rather than a crushing "pliers" type, which would be painful on a Shepherd's thick nails. Cut the tip of the nail, preferably when softened after a bath, taking care to avoid the sensitive quick. Always reward your dog for its good behavior.

WHERE TO CLIP NAILS
The pink nail bed, or quick, contains blood vessels and nerves, and is hidden by the Shepherd's black outer nail. To avoid cutting into it, ask your vet exactly where to clip.

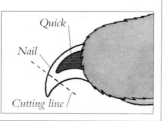

Quick

Nail

Cutting line

WASHING THE PAWS

After a country walk, clean your dog's muddy paws in a bowl filled with tepid or cool water. Avoid hot water, especially in cold weather. Using a mild soap suitable for human skin, rub your fingers between the pads to remove caked, hardened mud. Rinse and dry the paws thoroughly afterward.

ANAL HYGIENE

Excessive licking or dragging of the rear can mean that the scent-producing anal sacs are blocked, causing discomfort. Wearing protective gloves, squeeze the sacs empty, applying firm pressure from both sides. Use absorbent material to collect the fluid.

MAINTAINING THE COAT

REGULAR GROOMING IS ESSENTIAL to keep your Shepherd healthy and attractive. Give attention to standard coats at least weekly, and on alternate days during twice-yearly molts. Long coats require daily care while molting, and from time to time all dogs will have to endure a bath!

ROUTINE GROOMING FOR GERMAN SHEPHERDS

BRUSHING OUT TANGLES
Using a slicker brush, remove dead hair and untangle any mats or knots on the legs, chest, and tail. During molts, much hair will be shed from your Shepherd's woolly undercoat and hard, dense top coat.

REMOVING DEBRIS
A bristle brush will rid the coat of debris and loose hairs. If using a double-surfaced brush, apply the pin side gently to avoid damaging the skin. Always check for signs of inflammation, dandruff, or parasites.

"Fingers" of comb reach through coat to massage skin

Comb through feathering on legs, chest, and tail

MASSAGING THE SKIN
Draw a soft rubber "fingered" grooming device through the coat to stimulate production of natural oils, promoting a glossy, healthy sheen. Alternatively, simply massage with your fingers.

COMBING THE FEATHERS
Particularly on long-coated dogs, comb thoroughly through the feathery hair on the legs, chest, and tail to remove any remaining tangles or stray strands of hair.

Trim hairs between toes

TRIMMING THE PAWS

If the hair has grown long between the toes, trim it with blunt-ended scissors. This will help prevent foreign bodies such as grass seeds from lodging painfully in the paws.

Rub chamois cloth over entire body

Afterward, reward your dog with praise, active play, or food treats

SHINING THE COAT

Complete the grooming routine by smoothing the coat with a clean, dry chamois leather. This wipes any loose flakes of skin from the surface and creates a brilliant shine. Signal that grooming is finished with the release command "OK," then reward your dog's good behavior with lavish praise.

BATHING YOUR DOG

Keep water and shampoo away from dog's eyes and ears

1 Bathing is necessary after your Shepherd rolls in offensive substances, to treat a variety of skin conditions, or simply to revive the coat's natural luster. Use a non-slip mat in the bath for safety, and lather thoroughly with dog or baby shampoo and tepid to warm water. Bathe outdoors with a garden hose only in hot weather.

2 Clean the face with a cloth, then rinse off all shampoo, giving special attention under the legs and tail. Talk to your dog in a firm but gentle tone throughout.

3 Squeeze excess water from the coat and wrap your dog in a towel. Let it shake, then rub dry or use a hairdryer set to warm, not hot. Again, finish with words of praise.

ESTABLISH GROOMING AS A BASIC RITUAL

Grooming is comforting to most dogs, but some dominant individuals may resent it. Avoid this by introducing grooming routines as soon as you acquire your dog, as part of standard obedience. It should quickly learn to accept your actions as a sign of leadership. If your dog is strong-willed, command it to lie down and lift its leg to submit to grooming.

BASIC HEALTH

YOUR SHEPHERD DEPENDS on you for its good health. Since it cannot tell you that something is wrong, you must observe how your dog moves and behaves; any changes in activity or regular habits may be warning signs of problems. Arrange annual check-ups, and always use your veterinarian as a source of advice.

EASY, GRACEFUL MOVEMENT

German Shepherds move with a unique elegance, quite unlike any other breed. A healthy dog should walk, trot, and run fluidly and effortlessly. Difficulties lying down or getting up may indicate joint problems – not uncommon, especially in older dogs. Limping is a sign that one leg in particular hurts, and head bobbing while walking usually also means that a dog is in pain. Watch your Shepherd in its daily activities and be alert to any signs of discomfort or obvious loss of mobility.

SOUND APPETITE AND EATING HABITS

Eating and toilet routines adopted during puppyhood are normally maintained throughout life. Even slight changes can be a sign of ill health, and should be referred to your vet. A reduced appetite can simply indicate boredom, but may also signal illness. Asking for food but not eating it can mean tooth pain. So too can sloppy eating – with food being dropped, then picked up and eaten. A heightened appetite without weight gain can indicate a thyroid problem. Increased thirst is always important and may be a sign of infection or conditions such as diabetes and liver or kidney disease. Seek veterinary advice if your dog drinks excessively, or develops chronic diarrhea or constipation.

Excessive drinking is medically significant

REGULAR PREVENTATIVE CHECKS

Dogs that are vaccinated and have annual health check-ups tend to live longer than those that do not. Many conditions, such as splenic tumors, are not outwardly apparent, but may be diagnosed upon physical examination. Always inform your vet of any observed deviations in behavior; problems are easiest to treat if detected early. Later in your Shepherd's life, regular twice-yearly clinic visits may be recommended.

ACTIVE AND ALERT?

Canines are creatures of habit. If your dog does not get up when it usually does, moves slower, or is reluctant to play, it could be ill. A stoic Shepherd, however, may try to behave normally to please its owner, regardless. Observe your dog closely; if its actions seem even slightly strange, ask your vet's advice.

Using stethoscope, vet listens to heart and lung sounds

Shepherd sits comfortably on table and is content to be examined

MAKING VISITS TO THE VET FUN

Introduce your Shepherd to the veterinary clinic before it needs any treatment, so that it can have an investigative sniff and explore the premises. Ask your vet to give your dog a food treat while it is there, to make the next visit more appealing. Repeat trips can be made less of a hardship for you, too, by taking out insurance for your pet's health. This will ensure that you can benefit from the most sophisticated diagnostics and treatments.

CARING FOR THE ELDERLY DOG

Do not expect your dog to remain puppylike forever. With age, it will slow down and may become hard of hearing, even irritable at times. Be patient with its behaviour, and gentle in your handling. Create less physically demanding activities; older dogs still enjoy playing, but are less agile and energetic. Mental stimulation also helps keep the years at bay.

COMMON PROBLEMS

THE GERMAN SHEPHERD has classic anatomical proportions and a subsequently low incidence of medical problems related to physique. Nevertheless, its lush coat is a superb home for external parasites, while gastrointestinal complaints occur more frequently than in many other popular breeds.

SKIN PARASITES

Fleas are the most common external parasite, although rescued dogs and puppies may contract lice or mites. Ticks are a serious problem in specific areas and seasons.

FLEA INFESTATION
Flea bites cause irritation and scratching. Regularly inspect your dog's coat and use flea-control methods recommended by your vet.

EAR MITE
These microscopic pests burrow into the skin, which becomes very sore and itchy. Clean all bedding and apply special insecticidal shampoo.

OBVIOUS SIGNS OF DISCOMFORT

Check coat for dandruff and visible parasites

Chronic scratching does not always indicate fleas

Paws may also be chewed in response to irritation

SCRATCHING
Dogs often scratch because of parasites, but allergies or injuries can be additional causes. Always have any irritation checked by your vet, who will prescribe treatment, which may include a variety of medications, as well as changes in diet or grooming.

Paw is groomed excessively and may in turn become infected

PERSISTENT LICKING
All dogs lick to groom themselves, but some German Shepherds may do so obsessively, causing skin inflammation and hair loss. Called "lick granuloma" or "lick dermatitis," this exaggerated grooming disorder frequently responds well to antianxiety drugs; seek professional advice.

TYPICAL CANINE COMPLAINTS

With any breed, many health problems can be prevented. Routinely examine your dog's skin, ears, and teeth, and keep all essential vaccinations up to date.

Heartworm infestation can be a threat in certain regions; if your area is affected, give your Shepherd preventative medication during the appropriate season.

EAR CANAL

TEETH

INNER EAR

ESOPHAGUS

SPLEEN

KIDNEY

LIVER

STOMACH

INTESTINES

HIP JOINT

EAR DISORDERS
Although the Shepherd's ears are almost ideal, with wide canals and an erect shape allowing good air circulation, infections are not uncommon. Check the ears regularly for wax, odor, discharge, inflammation, and foreign bodies such as grass seeds.

TOOTH CHIPS AND FRACTURES
With large jaws yielding immense crushing power, German Shepherds often delight in chewing through branches and bones. This may be fun for your dog, but to avoid dental damage or mouth lacerations and punctures, try discouraging unsuitable play items.

INTESTINAL PARASITES
Intestinal worms and other internal parasites may cause weight loss, vomiting, or diarrhea with or without blood and mucus. A dull coat, bloated abdomen, or persistent dragging of the hindquarters can indicate worms. Ask your vet for advice on effective worm prevention.

GASTROINTESTINAL UPSETS
German Shepherds have an above-average incidence of gastrointestinal disorders, and this predisposition is perhaps associated with temperament. However, there are many possible causes of an "irritable bowel"; while diarrhea can be anxiety-related, it may also reflect a specific food allergy or a variety of other factors. It is best to avoid giving your dog heavy or strongly spiced meals.

PAINFUL STRAINS
Active breeds such as Shepherds are naturally more prone to muscle, ligament, tendon, and joint injuries. Torn ligaments occur most commonly in the knee, while the hip joint is also easily damaged.

BREED-SPECIFIC PROBLEMS

SELECTIVE BREEDING for desirable traits inevitably also concentrates potentially harmful genes. Because the German Shepherd has been studied so extensively, numerous inherited medical conditions are known to affect the breed. Testing for hereditary disorders, of the bone and blood particularly, can help ensure healthy offspring.

HIP DYSPLASIA

Partly hereditary but also related to obesity or vigorous exercise during puppyhood, this form of hip joint arthritis causes chronic pain and lameness. Veterinary associations and kennel clubs have developed valuable hip-testing schemes for breeding stock.

NORMAL HIPS
The hip is a basic ball-and-socket joint. In healthy hips like these, the head of the femur (ball) sits comfortably and securely in the acetabulum (socket) of the hipbone. Dogs screened for hip abnormalities are given ratings, which are listed on certificates that any responsible breeder will hold.

DYSPLASTIC JOINTS
This X ray of a German Shepherd with severe hip dysplasia shows shallow, rough hip sockets and abrasive femoral heads. Any movement of one against the other causes discomfort. Affected dogs may display thigh muscle wasting, and often "bunny hop" to diminish pain.

CHRONIC DEGENERATIVE RADICULOMYELOPATHY

More common in German Shepherds than in any other breed, chronic degenerative radiculo-myelopathy usually occurs in dogs over seven years old. Hind leg lameness is the first sign of this disease of the central nervous system, with walking becoming increasingly difficult as partial paralysis develops over a period of months. Although painless, the condition is incurable.

Hind paw not quickly returned to flat position is common symptom of degenerative disorder

OTHER DISORDERS COMMON IN GERMAN SHEPHERDS

Although Shepherds generally have sound, well-proportioned physiques, they are nevertheless susceptible to a number of medical conditions. Some ailments are hereditary and cannot be prevented, but treatment may help to alleviate symptoms.

PITUITARY DWARFISM
A hereditary inefficiency of the pituitary gland results in dwarf German Shepherds. Affected dogs appear normal from birth to eight weeks, then grow slowly, only reaching the size of a small terrier, and eventually becoming virtually hairless.

EXOCRINE PANCREATIC INSUFFICIENCY
In this inherited ailment, the pancreas fails to secrete essential digestive enzymes. Onset is usually before the age of three years, evidenced by a loss of body tone and weight, and the elimination of clay-colored feces revealing much undigested food.

BRAIN

PITUITARY GLAND

PANCREAS

BONE MARROW

SHOULDER JOINT

BLOOD DISEASES
At least five genetic blood disorders are known in Shepherds, where the bone marrow fails to manufacture vital blood-clotting factors. Hemophilia A is a gender-linked condition carried on the "X" chromosome. Von Willebrand's disease is more common – it may affect up to one in five Shepherds in North America. Clinical severity declines with age.

BONE AND JOINT PROBLEMS
Panosteitis, excessive long bone production, during puppyhood is a breed problem seen largely in North America; this painful condition typically eases with maturity. Osteochondrosis, a joint cartilage abnormality, is increasingly prevalent world-wide. The shoulders and elbows are most frequently afflicted, causing pain-induced lameness. Treatment often involves surgery.

FORESEEING DANGERS

OUR DAILY SURROUNDINGS can present many dangers for a dog. Be mindful of your Shepherd's natural inclinations, and supervise it closely to prevent mishaps. Never leave your dog alone in situations where it may imperil itself or others, and be prepared to avert and react to trouble.

ENSURING SAFETY WITH YOUR GERMAN SHEPHERD

OVERCOMING APPREHENSIVENESS

A fearful German Shepherd may snap defensively, but is more likely to run with worry, possibly putting itself in danger from road traffic. If your Shepherd is apprehensive of other animals, strangers, or unfamiliar noises, reduce its anxiety through remedial training. Be alert to hazards, and use a lead to maintain firm control whenever your dog or others nearby may be at risk.

Nervous Shepherd may bolt out of fear

Outgoing Labrador is seen as threat

CONTROLLING AN INQUISITIVE NATURE

Monitor your Shepherd carefully when off the lead. Adventurous, curious dogs are more prone to injury, and exploratory wanders or investigative digging can result in bites from wild animals, stings, and irritations caused by plants or insects. Keep your dog away from known dangers, and always carry a basic first aid kit to treat minor cuts and lacerations.

DEALING WITH AGGRESSION

Train your Shepherd to obey your command, and avoid situations that may be confrontational. If your dog accidentally or intentionally bites another dog or a person, both you and your pet could face legal redress. You may also be held responsible for property damage. Good training is a social duty and a preventative measure. You can also buy insurance for your dog's activities.

COMMON POISONS AND CONTAMINANTS

IF INGESTED		ACTION
Slug and snail bait Strychnine rat poison Illegal drugs Aspirin and other painkillers Sedatives and antidepressants	Warfarin rat poison Lead (batteries, etc.) Antifreeze	Examine the package and determine its contents. If the poison was swallowed within the last two hours, induce vomiting by giving a "ball" of wet salt, or 3% hydrogen peroxide by mouth. Consult your vet immediately.
Acid Dishwasher granules Paint remover or thinner Kerosene or gasoline Drain, toilet, or oven cleaner	Chlorine bleach Laundry detergents Wood preservatives Polishes	Do not induce vomiting. Give raw egg white, baking soda, charcoal powder, or olive oil by mouth. Apply a paste of baking soda to any burns in the mouth. Seek urgent medical advice from your veterinarian.
IF IN CONTACT WITH THE COAT		**ACTION**
Paint Tar Petroleum products Motor oil		Do not apply paint remover or concentrated biological detergents. Wearing protective gloves, rub plenty of liquid paraffin or vegetable oil into the coat. Bathe with warm, soapy water or baby shampoo. Rub in flour to help absorb the poison.
Anything other than paint, tar, petroleum products, and motor oil		Wearing protective gloves, flush the affected area for at least five minutes, using plenty of clean, tepid water. Then bathe the contaminated coat thoroughly with warm, soapy water or mild, non-irritating baby shampoo.

EMERGENCY TREATMENT

With any case of poisoning, look for signs of shock, and give essential first aid as required. Contact your vet or local poison-control center for specific advice, and begin home treatment as quickly as possible, preferably under professional guidance by telephone.

STORE ALL TOXINS SECURELY

German Shepherds, especially when young, are inveterate chewers. Keep all household, garden, and swimming-pool chemicals stored safely out of reach, and never give your dog an empty container as a toy, or it will regard all similar objects as play items – with potentially tragic results.

PROTECTION FROM ELECTRICAL HAZARDS

Puppies naturally gnaw anything, and often find the texture of electrical cords particularly appealing. Train your dog from an early age not to tamper with electrical apparatus, and reduce the risk of burns or electrocution by placing electrical cords out of reach or spraying them with bitter-tasting aerosol. Switch off sockets when not in use and, if possible, add protective covers. If your Shepherd does chew through a live cable, do not risk your own life. Turn off the main electricity supply before administering first aid.

EMERGENCY FIRST AID

A HOME FIRST-AID KIT IS ESSENTIAL for patching up minor injuries.
More serious emergencies are much less common, but
with an understanding of basic principles and
techniques such as artificial respiration and
cardiac massage, you could save your dog's life.

FIRST-AID PRINCIPLES AND BASIC EQUIPMENT

The fundamentals of human first aid also apply to dogs. Your objectives are to preserve life, prevent further injury, control damage, minimize pain and distress, promote healing, and get your dog safely to a veterinarian for professional care. Have a fully stocked first-aid kit handy and use it to treat minor wounds, once you are certain there are no more serious, life-threatening problems to deal with.

BANDAGE

BANDAGE

BANDAGE

COTTON WAD

ANTISEPTIC CREAM

THERMOMETER

TWEEZERS

SCISSORS

ADHESIVE TAPE

ADHESIVE BANDAGE

STERILE DRESSING

GAUZE

HOW TO ASSESS AN UNCONSCIOUS DOG

Causes of unconsciousness include choking, electrocution, near-drowning, poisoning, blood loss, concussion, shock, fainting, smoke inhalation, diabetes, and heart failure. If you find your dog apparently unconscious, call its name to see if it responds. Pinch hard between the toes, while checking the eyes for blinking. Pull on a limb – does your dog pull back? Put your hand firmly on its chest and feel for a heartbeat. Lift the lip and look at the color of the gums. If they are pink and when you squeeze the pinkness out it comes back immediately, your dog's heart is beating. If the gums are pale or blue, cardiac massage may be required.

Pale or blue gums may indicate life-threatening shock

Shock can either weaken or elevate the heart rate

ARTIFICIAL RESPIRATION AND CARDIAC MASSAGE

Do not attempt to give artificial respiration or heart massage unless your dog is unconscious and will die without your help. If your dog has been pulled from water, suspend it by its hind legs for at least 30 seconds to drain the air passages. If it has been electrocuted, do not touch it until the electricity is turned off. If it has choked, press over the ribs to dislodge object. Never put yourself at risk; if possible share first-aid procedures with someone else or have them telephone the nearest veterinarian and arrange transportation.

Tongue is pulled fully forward and debris removed

Hold muzzle shut and seal your mouth over dog's nostrils

1 Place your dog on its side, with its head slightly lower than the rest of its body, to send more blood to the brain. Clear the airway by straightening the neck, pulling the tongue forwards, and sweeping the mouth with two fingers to remove any saliva or obstructions. Also ensure that the nose is not clogged with mucus or debris. If you cannot hear the heart, start cardiac massage at once.

2 Close the mouth, hold the muzzle with both hands, and place your mouth around the nose. Blow in until you see the chest expand, then let the lungs deflate. Repeat this 10–20 times per minute, checking the pulse every 10 seconds to make sure the heart is beating.

ALWAYS LOOK FOR SHOCK

Shock is a potentially life-endangering condition which occurs when the body's circulation fails. It can be caused by vomiting, diarrhea, poisons, animal bites, a twisted stomach, bleeding, and many other illnesses or accidents, and onset may not be apparent for several hours. The signs include pale or blue gums, rapid breathing, a faint or quickened pulse, cold extremities, and general weakness. Treating shock takes precedence over other injuries, including fractures. Your priorities are to control any bleeding, maintain body heat, and support vital functions. Unless shock is the result of heatstroke, wrap your dog loosely in a warm blanket, elevate its hindquarters, stabilize breathing and the heart if necessary, and get urgent medical advice. If your dog begins to panic, try to prevent it from injuring itself further, and take care you are not bitten.

Pumping forces blood toward brain

3 If the heart has stopped, begin cardiac massage immediately. Place the heel of one hand on the left side of the chest just behind the elbow, then the heel of your other hand on top. Press vigorously down and forwards to push blood into the brain, pumping 80–100 times per minute. Alternate 20–25 cardiac massages with 10 seconds of mouth-to-nose respiration until the heart beats, then continue resuscitation until breathing starts. A very large Shepherd should be laid on its back and pressed on the breastbone for cardiac massage.

MINOR INJURY AND ILLNESS

EVERY OWNER SHOULD KNOW how to administer medicines and other basic treatment to their dog in the event of accident or illness. Injuries to ears and paws, from fights or sharp objects, are not uncommon, and may require prompt bandaging and precautionary restraint before a vet is called.

EMERGENCY EAR BANDAGE

1 While an assistant soothes and steadies your dog, apply clean, preferably non-stick, absorbent material to the wound. Cut a section from a pair of tights and slip it over your hands. Speak reassuringly as you give first aid. Be careful: fear may cause your dog to bite.

Assistant kneels behind, keeping injured dog still

2 With your assistant holding the absorbent pad in place, slip the tights over your dog's head. This pressure bandage will hold the ear firmly, helping the blood to clot.

3 If necessary, secure the tights at each end with adhesive tape to prevent your dog from removing the bandage with its paws. The final result provides excellent temporary cover, while also allowing air into the wound. However, you should visit your veterinarian as soon as possible for a thorough examination of the injury.

BANDAGING A WOUNDED PAW

With the aid of an assistant, calm and steady your dog. To control bleeding, apply fresh, non-stick, absorbent material to the cut, wrap the dressing in place with stretchy gauze, and secure it with a layer of adhesive bandage. Be careful not to wrap so tightly that circulation is inhibited, and consult your vet for antibiotics or possible surgery. Change bandages daily to reduce the risk of infection.

IMPROVISING A MUZZLE

Apply a muzzle for safety unless breathing is poor

1 Even the most loving animal is capable of accidentally biting when hurt. With an assistant holding your dog still, make a loop with any soft material such as tights, gauze, or a tie, and slip it over the muzzle.

GIVING A PILL

2 With the loop in place, tighten it gently. Then bring both lengths of material down and cross them under the jaws. If your dog is confused or upset, speak to it in a relaxed, comforting tone.

3 To complete the process, wrap the material around the back of the ears and knot the ends securely. With the muzzle fastened, you can then safely give attention to specific injuries elsewhere.

1 With your dog seated, open its mouth and insert the pill as far back as possible. Liquid medicines may be squirted into the mouth with a syringe.

USING AN ELIZABETHAN COLLAR

Your veterinarian may provide a lampshade-shaped collar for your convalescent Shepherd, to prevent any scratching or chewing at wounds. This collar should be left on whenever your dog is unattended, but may be removed at mealtimes or during exercise on a lead, when you can deter self-inflicted damage. The device is rather cumbersome and likely to be worn with considerable reluctance!

2 Close your dog's mouth and tilt its head up, stroking the neck to induce swallowing. Alternatively, hide a pill in a piece of meat to simplify the procedure.

ORIGINS OF THE BREED

THE WORLD'S MOST SUCCESSFUL dog-breeding program began in Germany at the turn of the century, with a dog named Horand, whose noble features and loyal, spirited character inspired his owner to establish a new breed. These same exceptional qualities have since made the German Shepherd a worldwide favorite.

THE FIRST GERMAN SHEPHERD

In 1899, a German cavalry officer, Max von Stephanitz, bought a five-year-old dog called Hektor at a small dog show. Enthused by the dog's fine looks and obedient yet zestful nature, he renamed it Horand von Grafrath and two weeks later, with Artur Meyer, founded the German Shepherd Club, the *Verein für deutsche Schäferhunde*, or SV. Horand, who had a short coat and was roughly 24 in (60 cm) tall – small by today's standards – was the first registered German Shepherd. The SV remains the world's largest breed club.

HORAND VON GRAFRATH

NEAREST RELATIVES

During the late 1800s in southern Belgium, The Netherlands, and northern Germany, there existed a variety of herding and livestock-guarding dogs. While the closely related Belgian and Dutch Shepherds still have many classifications, German Shepherds were all bred to the SV standard set by Captain von Stephanitz. In this century, the German Shepherd has been used as the basic stock for the development of newer breeds.

GROENENDAEL (BELGIAN)
Long, feathery coat and slim, elongated muzzle

TERVUEREN (BELGIAN)
Almost extinct at end of World War II

MALINOIS (BELGIAN)
Closest in appearance to German Shepherd

SHILOH SHEPHERD
*From 1980s onward,
selectively bred from
German Shepherds in
United States for good
hips, large size, and
calm disposition*

DUTCH SHEPHERD (LONG-HAIRED)
*Less common than Belgian Shepherd, other
Dutch varieties have short or wiry coats*

**SAARLOOS
WOLFHOUND**
*First developed in
The Netherlands in
1920s by crossing
German Shepherd
with Canadian
timber wolf*

CZECH WOLFDOG
*Since 1950s, bred in
former Czechoslovakia
as cross of German
Shepherd and local
Carpathian wolf*

MYTH OF THE "WOLF COUSIN"

The German Shepherd's imposing stature, dark coat
coloring, and striking looks have led some people to
believe that it was developed with the addition of
wolf blood lines. This is not so. The breed evolved
from dogs that are perhaps a thousand generations
distant from their common wolf ancestor. Through
natural selective breeding, the Shepherd's appearance
was gradually altered to resemble that of the wolf.
Experiments in crossbreeding German Shepherds
with wolves have resulted in dogs that
are more nervous, and far less trainable
and responsive than purebred
German Shepherds.

REPRODUCTION

PRODUCING A LITTER of German Shepherd puppies is in itself easy, since both male and female Shepherds are naturally good breeders. However, the decision to mate your dog must be made responsibly – with professional guidance, and the best interest of the breed at heart.

THE MATING INSTINCT

Healthy males as young as 10 months can be used for mating. It is best to wait until a female is about two years old, in roughly her third estrous cycle, when she is emotionally prepared for a litter. Ovulation usually occurs 10-12 days after the first sign of bleeding and vulvar swelling. The most successful matings generally take place on the male's home turf.

PREGNANCY DIAGNOSIS

Ovulation, the optimum time to mate, is accurately indicated by an increased level of the hormone progesterone in the blood. Pregnancy, however, cannot be confirmed by blood or urine tests. Ultrasound at three weeks or a physical examination slightly later remain the best means of diagnosis.

Ultrasound scan shows several puppies in womb

DEALING WITH MISMATING

Mismatings can be avoided by keeping a watchful eye on your bitch when in season, by using tablets or injections to prevent ovulation, or by spaying. If an unwanted mating does occur, contact your vet. A pregnancy can be terminated, usually within three days of mating, with a hormone injection. This will induce an immediate repeat season, demanding renewed vigilance for 8–15 days after the beginning of vaginal discharge.

SPECIAL NEEDS OF AN EXPECTANT BITCH

During the first month of pregnancy, a bitch should continue to exercise freely. Thereafter, the increasing weight of the litter will naturally make her slower and less agile. After the sixth week, food intake should be gradually increased so that by the expected delivery date, she will be eating 30 percent more than normal. Provide a proper balance of calcium and phosphorus in the diet to promote strong bone growth.

MALE AND FEMALE REPRODUCTIVE SYSTEMS

A bitch comes into season twice yearly, is fertile for three days during each cycle, and will be receptive to mating only during these periods. Males, however, willingly mate year-round. For the female, ovulation continues throughout life and there is no menopause, although breeding in later years is risky. Pregnancy lasts for about 63 days.

RESPONSIBLE BREEDING

If planning to breed your Shepherd, seek professional advice from your vet or from an experienced and reputable breeder. Ensure that the prospective parents' physical and emotional attributes will enhance the breed. Both partners should be screened for certain inherited diseases such as hip dysplasia, detected by X ray. Your vet may also advise testing for brucellosis, a canine venereal disease. Remember that it is unfair to bring a litter of puppies into the world that will be unwanted or ill; it is up to you to find each offspring a safe home.

PREVENTING PREGNANCY

Neutering is the most effective and safest means of preventing pregnancy. The female, because she carries the young, is the usual candidate. Both the ovaries and the uterus are removed, followed by a week's rest. The procedure for males is less complicated, involving a small incision to the scrotum for removal of the testicles.

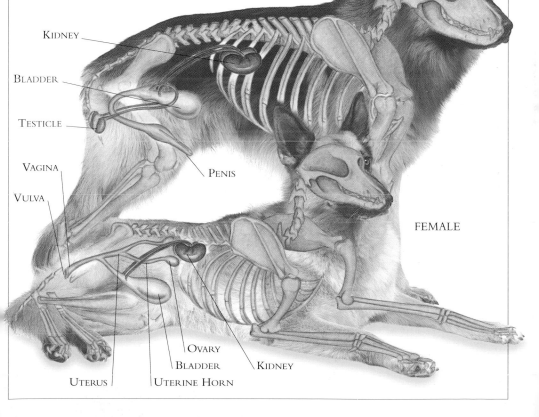

MALE

KIDNEY

BLADDER

TESTICLE

VAGINA

VULVA

PENIS

FEMALE

OVARY

BLADDER

KIDNEY

UTERUS

UTERINE HORN

PRE- AND POST-WHELPING

AS THE DAY OF BIRTH approaches, introduce the expectant mother to her whelping box and arrange for your vet to be on call in case of problems. Although Shepherds seldom have difficulties, it is best to have experienced help both at the delivery and later, for aftercare of weak puppies.

INTRODUCING A WHELPING BOX

Several weeks before she is due to deliver, familiarize the mother-to-be with her whelping box. The box should have a length and width of at least 4 ft (1.2 m), and be made of plywood, which will not be damaged by birth fluids. Three sides should be 18–20 in (45–50 cm) high to prevent the puppies from wandering off; the fourth should have a lockable opening to allow the mother easy access. Start collecting newspaper; you will need several bundles to line the box and to serve as bedding for the new puppies for the next two months.

Expectant mother feels secure in her specially made whelping "den"

DELIVERY CARE

If you have never been present at a birth, ask an experienced dog breeder to attend, and inform your vet when labor begins. Keep the room temperature at around 77° F (25° C). If after two hours your bitch does not produce a puppy, contact your vet once again for advice. The puppy's position may need manipulating to facilitate delivery. Although uncommon, some Shepherds do require a Cesarean section. Place a warm, towel-covered hot-water bottle in a cardboard box, and keep this nearby as a safe receptacle for each newly delivered puppy. The box may also be used to carry the puppies if mother and litter need to be taken to the vet.

SIGNS OF IMPENDING BIRTH

Your bitch is likely to refuse food shortly before she goes into labor. She will restlessly seek out her whelping box and start to tear up the bedding, preparing a nest for her puppies. Her body temperature will drop, and she may pant. When her water breaks and contractions begin, birth is imminent. Avoid distractions and keep other animals and strangers away while the bitch is in labor.

THE NEW LITTER

Towel-dry each puppy after it is delivered and clear its nose of mucus; all newborns should squeal and wriggle. During whelping, offer the mother warm milk. Let her rest after labor has ended and all placentas have been delivered. Place each puppy by a teat to suckle. The bitch will also need plenty of food in the coming weeks – at peak lactation, up to four times her normal intake.

Young puppies suckle greedily

ASSISTING A WEAK OR ABANDONED PUPPY

HELPING TO SUCKLE

On average, one out of seven puppies is born relatively small and weak. Runts are often the least healthy of the litter, and if left to nature frequently die within a few days. To aid survival, place a frail puppy near the teats offering the best supply of milk.

BOTTLE-FEEDING

In large, healthy litters where there simply is not enough milk to feed all the puppies, or when the mother is incapacitated or abandons her offspring, use canine milk formula as a supplement. Bottle-feed initially every two to three hours, seeking your vet's guidance on the correct quantities.

BRINGING UP THE BROOD

From three weeks of age, the maturing puppies begin to explore; by 12 weeks, the senses are fully developed. Handle and groom all puppies frequently, so they learn to accept being touched by humans, but be careful not to upset the mother, who will be protective. Gentle exposure to new sights and sounds during this early period will help the puppies to grow into well-adjusted, adaptable adults.

Puppies rely on mother for first three weeks of life

Puppies crawl from birth

PREPARING FOR A SHOW

TAKING PART IN a dog show can be great fun, but both you and your Shepherd should be fully prepared. Teach your dog show manners, and make sure it is in prime condition, as it will be judged against a breed standard of ideal physical and personality characteristics typifying the "perfect" specimen.

BASIC EQUIPMENT FOR YOU AND YOUR DOG

FOR HANDLING AND SECURITY

You will need a nonchoke show collar that permits the judge to have an unimpeded view of your dog's neck, and a slim lead about 5 ft (1.5 m) long. If attending a "benched" event, take a benching chain to secure your dog in its allotted space, as well as an identification number clip.

COLLAR AND NAME TAG

NUMBER CLIP

BENCHING CHAIN

SHOW LEAD

TRANSPORTATION AND SUPPLIES

Your dog will travel best in a crate loaded in the back of a car. Pack food and water for your dog, along with its bowls. If you plan to picnic, also take refreshments for yourself. Folding chairs and a large umbrella for sun or rain protection are essential, as are plastic bags or a "poop scoop" to clear up your dog's mess. A towel is useful for cleaning muddy paws. Keep all supplies, including grooming equipment, in a designated bag for show use.

MEETING SHOW STANDARDS

Visit shows alone first to see exactly what occurs. While working trials require dogs well-trained in obedience and a variety of specialized skills, kennel club events demand only beauty and personality. For these, your dog's coat must be in good condition, its ears clear of wax, and the teeth tartar-free. Bathe your dog and clip its nails a few days before a show, to allow renewal of the coat's gloss by natural oils. No cosmetic aids to improve a dog's appearance are permitted at shows.

Soft chamois mitt is used to shine coat

Training and Temperament for the Ring

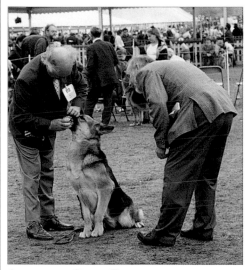

Adopting a Correct Stance
Seek advice from a professional breeder on training your dog to stand correctly in the show ring. This is one of the curious rituals of formal exhibition. Judges respond best to dogs that are placed in and stay in the show position, which allows the top line, hind legs, and head of your Shepherd to be thoroughly inspected and assessed.

Shepherd's head is held high

Hind legs are positioned so that both are visible in profile

801

Accepting Close Examination
A successful show dog has been trained from puppyhood to accept being scrutinized by strangers. Reward your dog for permitting unfamiliar people to handle it as a judge would – allowing the hindquarters to be touched, and the mouth to be opened and the teeth examined. Judges invariably prefer dogs that are amenable as well as handsome.

Excitement of Participating

A dog show is exciting for owners because of the hope of winning, and exciting for canines because it is an opportunity to meet many other dogs. Without early and continued training, some dogs become over-eager and are more intent on interacting with other dogs than on performing in the ring. Train your German Shepherd to be relaxed in the presence of other dogs, and calm and reassure it before entering the ring.

Costs of Showing

Showing your German Shepherd can be inexpensive, or surprisingly costly. If you show your own dog, your only expenses are entry fees, transportation, and accommodation. At higher levels on the show circuit, professional handlers are frequently used. This can add a very considerable financial burden, and it is a rare dog that is so successful that handling costs are earned back in stud fees or puppy prices. If you are not interested in serious exhibiting, a more sensible approach to showing your Shepherd is to consider it a pleasurable pastime for both you and your dog.

WHAT HAPPENS AT A SHOW

EXHIBITING EVENTS RANGE from informal local competitions, to open shows for all breeds, to exclusive Shepherd championships. Each has its own rules, but all follow similar principles in the quest to find a truly outstanding dog. Shows can provide a very sociable and rewarding day out for owners and canines alike.

SETTLING IN AT THE BENCHES

At some shows, dogs are housed at numbered "benches." Secure your dog with a benching chain and offer it a drink of water. Have someone stay at the bench so your dog does not become bored, and postpone meals until after it is shown to keep it active and alert.

Last-minute combing takes care of any disarray

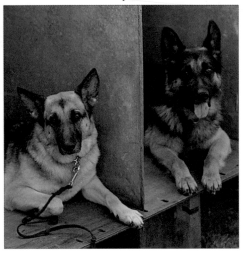

GROOMING FOR THE RING

Just before entering the show ring, give your dog a final groom so that it looks its absolute best; this can also be calming for both of you. It is wise to take your dog to relieve itself too.

Owner holds dog gently while it is being examined

STANDING FOR INSPECTION

When called, enter the ring and set your dog in its "show stance." The judge will examine the body in detail to see how closely it conforms to the breed standard. During the inspection, interfere as little as possible, but keep the head held high for proper presentation. Your dog's temperament is being noted too, and any nervousness, resistance, or aggression will be viewed unfavorably.

RELAXING IN THE EXCITEMENT

Shows are competitive, but many owners view them as an enjoyable hobby offering the chance to socialize with like-minded people and to have a pleasant outing with their dogs.

LINEUP OF FINALISTS

After the individual assessments, a short list of five or six dogs is chosen and inspected once again. The judge will then place the finalists in order of merit, awarding ribbons for first, second, and third place, as well as for "reserve" and "highly commended" contenders.

ASSESSMENT OF THE GAIT

The judge will ask for each dog to be walked around the ring, to appraise its movement. Dogs should "gait" with confidence and fluid grace; a stilted or hesitant manner will be penalized. Symmetry between dog and handler is also important. Some Shepherds are natural show-offs and relish parading in the limelight, while others find it all rather boring.

Legs should flow effortlessly beneath a firm back

BEST OF BREED

Winning dogs have the physical attributes of a champion along with a "star" personality. It is a great achievement if your Shepherd has captured a prize. Yet ideal looks and show style are not the sole criteria of an outstanding dog; any Shepherd in glowing health and with a fine temperament is just as much a winner.

SPECIALIZED TRAINING

THE GERMAN SHEPHERD is among the most versatile and successful of all breeds – obedient, agile, and exceptionally responsive to commands. Shepherds can be trained to high standards to excel in competitive working trials, while their courageous, protective nature also makes them a popular security and police dog.

POLICE AND SECURITY DUTIES

PATROL AND DEFENSE ROLES

Many breeds have been used by both private and public organizations as security dogs, yet the dependable German Shepherd has usually emerged the favorite. At one time, Shepherds were trained by inflicting pain. Today, most professional security forces use less aggressive methods, producing more steady but equally effective guard dogs. Barking at unexpected noises or strangers is central to training.

ASSISTANT OFFICER ON THE BEAT

The Shepherd's watchful, loyal nature and supreme responsiveness to commands make it ideal for police work, where dog and handler operate on a system of mutual trust. Some canine "cops" have even been equipped for duty with video cameras so that the handler sees exactly what the dog sees. Usually, police dogs are taught to retrieve rather than attack; training begins with fetching a padded wooden "arm" and finishes with retrieving a "villain" by the arm. A Shepherd trained in this manner is completely reliable, and can be petted by children on a crowded street one minute, and chase and capture a culprit the next.

ADVANCED OBEDIENCE TRIALS

RETRIEVING A DUMBBELL

Competitive obedience trials provide good mental stimulation. Begin classes at six months, after your dog has mastered walking on a lead and basic commands. Advanced training includes close and fast-pace heelwork, retrieves, recalls, distant control, sustained sit/downs (at times with the handler out of sight), and scent discrimination.

SEND-AWAY COMMAND

A higher-level obedience skill is the "send-away," where a dog is sent into a square area, commanded to turn and lie down facing its owner, then to return. Dogs also learn to stay down unattended for as long as 10 minutes.

TRAINING IN AGILITY

CLIMBING A LADDER

Agility courses open to all dogs are run "against the clock." Although the German Shepherd is not as fast as some other breeds, it is very nimble and performs with the best. Climbing a ladder is a sophisticated test of agility used only in police dog-training programs.

JUMPING HURDLES

Agility work requires dexterity, confidence, and instant response to command, and can be an excellent channel for restless energy. Standard trial apparatus includes an "A" frame, hurdles, a tire, poles to weave through, a tunnel, and a seesaw. Training demands ample patience; start when your dog is a year old by enrolling in a local club.

ASSISTANCE ROLES

ALTHOUGH A RELATIVELY new breed – developed this century – the German Shepherd already has a magnificent record of service. From initial work in the fields of war, these able dogs have been employed for police and security duties, to assist the disabled, and in scent tracking for search and rescue or detection roles.

A DISTINGUISHED HISTORY OF SERVICE

In the early 1900s the German Shepherd's role was as a farm worker, but World War I created new needs which the adaptable Shepherd aptly filled. It served as a Red Cross dog searching for wounded soldiers and carrying first-aid equipment, and was a battlefield messenger, telephone cable layer, sentry, and defender of ammunition dumps. At the end of the war, British and American army personnel took Shepherds home. Because it was known as a German dog, British breeders changed the name to Alsatian Wolf Dog, and then simply Alsatian. The Shepherd expanded its services under that name, which survived until the 1970s.

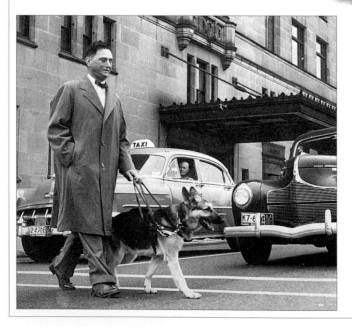

FIRST GUIDE DOGS

Following World War I, the German government trained Shepherds to act as eyes for blinded soldiers. Guide-dog training was furthered in Switzerland and from there, in the 1930s, the concept was exported to France, Britain, and North America. Pictured here is Buddy III, among the first official guide dogs brought to the United States from Switzerland. By the 1950s the Shepherd was the world's most popular dog for assisting the blind. In many countries it remains the guide-dog breed of choice.

TRAINED FOR ASSISTANCE WORK

German Shepherds are selectively bred for good health and the necessary temperament for guide-dog work. Initial training during puppyhood is often conducted in the homes of volunteers. Formal instruction then follows at a specialized training center, where the dog is taught to see and think for its blind owner, warning of obstacles or dangers. Owners also receive training to understand their individual guide dog.

SEARCH AND RESCUE ROLES

In earthquakes and avalanches, search and rescue Shepherds trained to follow ground and air scent trails perform superbly. Many also work in mountainous regions, locating people lost in fog or unknown terrain. The dogs draw attention to humans buried in snow or debris by digging or barking.

IDEAL POLICE PARTNER

Police and security forces employ the Shepherd as a multi-purpose worker – in search and rescue, scent tracking, defense, and some forms of attack. Each dog and handler operate as a team. Ideally, the handler acquires his dog as a puppy and raises it with his own family, teaching it basic obedience with the help of the police training school. Once the dog is fully mature, the team enters full-time training at the school. Training and assessment continue throughout the dog's working career. Dogs often finally retire to their handlers' homes.

SCENT TRACKING

Government and other agencies often use German Shepherds to detect contraband, illicit drugs, explosives, and other prohibited items at borders, airports, and harbors, working both on open land and in buildings.

BREED STANDARD

A BREED STANDARD is used by the governing kennel club of each country to describe the ideal German Shepherd. Show dogs are judged against this formal index of the unique physical qualities, demeanor, and personality traits that characterize a "perfect" specimen of the breed.

GERMAN SHEPHERD DOG
HERDING GROUP
(Last revised February 1978)

Adopted by the German Shepherd Dog Club of America and approved by the American Kennel Club. Reprinted with permission.

GENERAL APPEARANCE The first impression of a good German Shepherd Dog is that of a strong, agile, well-muscled animal, alert and full of life. It is well balanced, with harmonious development of the forequarter and hindquarter. The dog is longer than tall, deep-bodied and presents an outline of smooth curves rather than angles. It looks substantial and not spindly, giving the impression, both at rest and in motion, of muscular fitness and nimbleness without any look of clumsiness or soft living. The ideal dog is stamped with a look of quality and nobility – difficult to define, but unmistakable when present. Secondary sex characteristics are strongly marked and every animal gives a definite impression of masculinity or femininity, according to its sex.

CHARACTER The breed has a distinct personality marked by direct and fearless, but not hostile, expression, self-confidence, and a certain aloofness that does not lend itself to immediate and indiscriminate friendships. The dog must be approachable, quietly standing its ground and showing confidence and willingness to meet overtures without itself making them. It is poised, but when the occasion demands, eager and alert; both fit and willing to serve in its capacity as companion, watchdog, blind leader, herding dog, or guardian, whichever the circumstances may demand. The dog must not be timid, shrinking behind its master or handler; it should not be nervous, looking about or upward with anxious expression or showing nervous reactions, such as tucking of tail, to strange sounds or sights. Lack of confidence under any surroundings is not typical of good character. Any of the above deficiencies in character, which indicate shyness must be penalized as very serious faults, and any dog exhibiting pronounced indications of these must be excused from the ring. It must be possible for the judge to observe the teeth and to determine that both testicles are descended. *Any dog that attempts to bite the judge must be disqualified.* The ideal dog is a working animal with an incorruptible character combined with body and gait suitable for the arduous work which constitutes its primary purpose.

HEAD The head is noble, cleanly chiseled, strong without coarseness, but above all not fine, and in proportion to its body. The head of the male is distinctly masculine, and that of the bitch distinctly feminine. The muzzle [the head in front of the eyes, nasal bone, nostrils, and jaws; the foreface] is long and strong with the lips firmly fitted, and its top line is parallel to the top line of the skull. Seen from the front, the forehead is only moderately arched, and the skull slopes into the long, wedge-shaped muzzle without abrupt stop [the step up from muzzle to skull; the indentation between the eyes where the nasal bone and skull meet]. Jaws are strongly developed.

EARS Ears are moderately pointed, in proportion to the skull, open toward the front, and carried erect when at attention, the ideal carriage being one in which the center lines of the ears, viewed from the front, are parallel to each other and perpendicular to the ground. *A dog with cropped [the cutting or trimming of the ear leather for the purpose of inducing the ears to stand erect] or hanging ears must be disqualified.*

EYES Of medium size, almond shaped, set a little obliquely and not protruding. The color is as dark as possible. The expression keen, intelligent, and composed.

TEETH 42 in number – 20 upper and 22 lower – are strongly developed and meet in a scissors bite in which part of the inner surface of the upper incisors meet and engage part of the outer surface of the lower incisors. An over shot jaw [the front teeth of the upper jaw overlap and do not touch the front teeth of the lower jaw when the mouth is closed] or a level bite is undesirable. *An under shot jaw [the front teeth of the lower jaw projecting beyond the front teeth of the upper jaw when the mouth is closed] is a disqualifying fault.* Complete dentition is to be preferred. Any missing teeth other than first premolars is a serious fault.

NECK The neck is strong and muscular, clean-cut and relatively long, proportionate in size to the head and without loose folds of skin. When the dog is at attention or excited, the head is raised and the neck carried high, otherwise typical carriage of the head is forward rather than up but a little higher than the top of the shoulders, particularly in motion.

FOREQUARTERS The shoulder blades are long and obliquely angled, laid on flat and not placed forward. The upper arm joins the shoulder blade at about a right angle. Both the upper arm and the shoulder blade are well muscled. The forelegs, viewed from all sides, are straight and the bone oval rather than round. The pasterns [the region of the foreleg between the carpus or wrist and the digits] are strong and springy and angulated at approximately a 25 degree angle from the vertical.

FEET The feet are short, compact, with toes well arched, pads thick and firm, nails short and dark. The dewclaws [the fifth digit on the inside of the legs], if any, should be removed from the hind legs. Dewclaws on the forelegs may be removed, but are normally left on.

PROPORTION The German Shepherd Dog is longer than tall, with the most desirable proportion as 10 to 8½. The desired height for males at the top of the highest point of the shoulder blade is 24 to 26 inches; and for bitches 22 to 24 inches. The length is measured from the point of the prosternum or breastbone to the rear edge of the pelvis, the ischial tuberosity.

BODY The whole structure of the body gives an impression of depth and solidity without bulkiness. *Chest* – Commencing at the prosternum, it is well filled and carried well down between the legs. It is deep and capacious, never shallow, with ample room for lungs and heart, carried well forward, with the prosternum showing ahead of the shoulder in profile. *Ribs* – Well sprung and long, neither barrel-shaped nor too flat, and carried down to a sternum which reaches to the elbows. Correct ribbing allows the elbows to move back freely when the dog is at a trot. Too round causes interference and throws the elbows out, too flat or short causes pinched elbows. Ribbing is carried well back so that the loin is relatively short. *Abdomen* – Firmly held and not paunchy. The bottom line is only moderately tucked up in the loin.

TOPLINE *Withers* – The withers [the highest point of the body, immediately behind the neck] are higher than and sloping into the level back. *Back* – The back is straight, very strongly developed without sag or roach [a convex curvature of the back toward the loin], and relatively short. The desirable long proportion is not derived from a long back, but from overall length with relation to height, which is achieved by length of forequarter and length of withers and hindquarter, viewed from the side. *Loin* – [the region of the body on either side of the vertebral column between the last ribs and the hindquarters]. Viewed from the top, broad and strong. Undue length between the last rib and the thigh, when viewed from the side, is undesirable. *Croup* – [also known as the rump – the part of the back from the front of the pelvis to the root of the tail]. Long and gradually sloping. *Tail* – Bushy with the last vertebrae extended at least to the hock joint [the tarsus or collection of bones of the hind leg forming the joint between the second thigh and the metatarsus]. It is set smoothly into the croup and low rather than high. At rest, the tail hangs in a slight curve like a saber. A slight hook, sometimes carried to one side, is faulty only to the extent that it mars general appearance. When the dog is excited or in motion, the curve is accentuated and the tail raised, but it should never be curled forward beyond a vertical line. Tails too short, or with clumpy ends due to ankylosis, are serious faults. *A dog with a docked [shortened by cutting] tail must be disqualified.*

HINDQUARTERS The whole assembly of the thigh, viewed from the side, is broad, with both upper and lower thigh well muscled, forming as nearly as possible a right angle. The upper thigh bone parallels the shoulder blade while the lower thigh bone parallels the upper arm. The metatarsus (the unit between the hock joint and the foot) is short, strong, and tightly articulated.

GAIT A German Shepherd Dog is a trotting dog, and its structure has been developed to meet the requirements of its work. *General Impression* – The gait is outreaching, elastic, seemingly without effort, smooth and rhythmic, covering the maximum amount of ground with the minimum number of steps. At a walk it covers a great deal of ground, with long strides of both hind legs and forelegs. At a trot the dog covers still more ground with even longer stride, and moves powerfully but easily, with co-ordination and balance so that the gait appears to be the steady motion of a well-lubricated machine. The feet travel close to the ground on both forward reach and backward push. In order to achieve ideal movement of this kind, there must be good muscular development and ligamentation. The hindquarters deliver, through the back, a powerful forward thrust which slightly lifts the whole animal and drives the body forward. Reaching far under, and passing the imprint left by the front foot, the hind foot takes hold of the ground; then hock, stifle [the joint of the hind leg between the thigh and the second thigh – the dog's knee] and upper thigh come into play and sweep back, the stroke of the hind leg finishing with the foot still close to the ground in a smooth follow through. The over reach of the hindquarter usually necessitates one hind foot passing outside and the other hind foot passing inside the track of the forefeet, and such action is not faulty unless the locomotion is crabwise with the dog's body sideways out of the normal straight line. *Transmission* – The typical smooth, flowing gait is maintained with great strength and firmness of back. The whole effort of the hindquarter is transmitted to the forequarter through the loin, back and withers. At full trot, the back must remain firm and level without sway, roll, whip, or roach. Unlevel topline with withers lower than the hip is a fault. To compensate for the forward motion imparted by the hindquarters, the shoulder should open to its full extent. The forelegs should reach out close to the ground in a long stride in harmony with that of the hindquarters. The dog does not track on widely separated parallel lines, but brings the feet inward toward the middle line of the body when trotting in order to maintain balance. The feet track closely but do not strike nor cross over. Viewed from the front, the front legs function from the shoulder joint to the pad in a straight line. Viewed from the rear, the hind legs function from the hip joint to the pad in a straight line. Faults of gait, whether from front, rear or side, are to be considered very serious faults.

COLOR The German Shepherd Dog varies in color, and most colors are permissible. Strong rich colors are preferred. Nose black. Pale, washed-out colors and blues and livers are serious faults. *A white dog or a dog with a nose that is not predominantly black, must be disqualified.*

COAT The ideal dog has a double coat [an outer coat resistant to weather, together with an undercoat of softer hair for warmth and waterproofing] of medium length. The outer coat should be as dense as possible, hair straight, harsh and lying close to the body. A slightly wavy outer coat, often of wiry texture, is permissible. The head, including the inner ear and foreface, and the legs and paws are covered with short hair, and the neck with longer thicker hair. The rear of the forelegs and hind legs has somewhat longer hair extending to the pastern and hock, respectively. Faults in coats include soft, silky, too long, outer coat, woolly, curly, and open coat.

INDEX

ACKNOWLEDGMENTS

AUTHOR'S ACKNOWLEDGMENTS

Many thanks to all those who were involved in the production of this handbook, with particular gratitude to Patricia Holden White for choreographing several photographic sessions, the Murkett family for lending me their excellent library of vintage German Shepherd books, Gary Clayton Jones for supplying X rays, Peter Kertesz for lending photographs of teeth, Ake Hedhammar in Sweden for help with translations and for finding photos of Horand, the first registered German Shepherd, and Ivan Gerger at the Waltham Centre of Pet Nutrition for providing advice on the German Shepherd's energy requirements.

PUBLISHER'S ACKNOWLEDGMENTS

Dorling Kindersley would like to thank photographer Tracy Morgan for her invaluable contribution to the book. Also special thanks to Tracy's photographic assistants: Sally Bergh-Roose, Stella Smyth-Carpenter, and Christina Hale. We are also very grateful to Patricia Holden White for her generous advice and help on photographic sessions. Thanks also to Karin Woodruff for the index, and to Sarah Kendall of The Company of Animals for supplying props. Finally, we would like to thank the following people for lending their dogs and/or for modeling:

Mitchell Andrews; Laurence Bard (Thunder); Wendy Bartlet; Roy and Maureen Beech (Rosie); Sally Bergh-Roose (Olderhill Abeth at Sarsway CDX UDX WDX TDX "Chaos," Sarsway Arak CDX UDX WD "Hudson," Sarsway Ardent CDX UD WD "Mallik," Yuarana Wild Joker "Rion," and Standahl Orie "Kes"; Allan and Marion Botchinsky (Theo); Ken, Chris, and Sheryl Brooks (Pepsi); Penny Carpanini (Tabathas Mirth "Mirth"); Connor and Judy Carroll (Oscar); Suzanne Collins (Karma); Bruce Fogle; Jill Fornary; David and Shantie Forrest (Lexter Jobey "Zack," Davantie Klamity Jane "Chloe," and the Davantie litter); Denise Frick (Bonnie Blue); Sarah and Victoria Goodwin; Christina Hale; Gillian Jane (Heelakeary Countess and her litter); Helen Lamb (Sabre); Sarah Lillicrapp; Hilary Lynette of the Conquell Dog Training Centre (Conquell Troila, Conquell Orrie, and Conquell Platz); Denise Murkett (Luke); Neil McAuliffe of Crown Protection Services Limited (Guinness, Murco, and Kelly); Tracy Morgan (Topkyri The Fire Dragon "Scorch"); Seán O'Connell; Valentine Olubodun; Mr. W. and Mrs. J. Petrie

(Champion Bilnetts Dirty Harry, Bilnetts Lucky Charm, and the Bilnetts "N" litter); Ken and Anita Plaster of the Aylesbury German Shepherd Dog Training Club (Heelacullum Breen of Heelakeary "Bonnie," Heelakeary Arno "Dancer," and Heelakeary Baron "Lieka"); Anne Price (Flora and Marla); Nick Roeg (Anna); Jane Russell; Juette Shallow; Hester Small; Stella and Stephanie Smyth-Carpenter (Dinah).

PHOTOGRAPHIC CREDITS

Key: l=left, r=right, t=top, c=center, a=above, b=below

All photography by Tracy Morgan except:
Animal Photography: (Sally Anne Thompson) 7cr, 17br, 73br, 74tl; **Jane Burton**: 56b; **Christopher Bradbury**: 64cr; **Mary Evans Picture Library**: 62cl, 74cr, 74bl; **Guide Dogs for the Blind Association**: 75tr; **The Image Bank**: (Lynn M. Stone) 6tl, (Joseph Van Os) 63br; **Impact Photos**: (Marilyn Greene) 75cl; **Microscopix Photo Library**: 52bl; **Rex Features**: (James Morgan) 72br, 72bl, 75bl, (Sipa Press) 75br; **Tim Ridley**: 4–5br, 7b, 8bl, 8br, 14cr, 14tl, 15c, 15tr, 22bl, 28–29, 33b, 42–43, 44bl, 44br, 44cr, 45bl, 45br, 46bl, 46c, 47br, 47tl, 49bl, 50b, 52t, 53, 56cr, 60b, 61bl, 61br, 61tl, 68cr, 70t; **Solitaire Photography**: 72ar, 73bl; **David Ward**: 7t, 18cl, 36bl, 37b; **Zefa Pictures**: 2.

ILLUSTRATIONS

Samantha Elmhurst: 53, 55, 65; **Sean Milne**: 58–59; **Jane Pickering**: 35; **Clive Spong**: 11.